HEALING SCHOOL
LEVEL 1 WORKBOOK
Amazing Love Healing Ministry
www.amazinglovehealing.com

Sharon L. Gottfried Lewis

XULON PRESS

Copyright © 2016 by Sharon Lynn Gottfried Lewis

Healing School Level 1 Workbook
A Course in Inner Healing
by Sharon Lynn Gottfried Lewis

Printed in the United States of America.
Edited by Xulon Press.

ISBN 9781498476119

www.xulonpress.com

Dedicated to my mentor in the Christian healing ministry, Dr. Rita Bennett, Christian Renewal Association, ministry, Dr. Rita Bennett, who initially invested in me her time, knowledge, and friendship, covering me with her prayers. I am grateful for all who have mentored me by relationship, writings, prayers, and teachings. To God I give all the glory!

Forward

I am so excited that you are reading this forward to The Rev'd Dr. Sharon Lewis' workbook for her Healing School I, because it means you are on a healing journey. I've been on the same journey myself and Pastor Sharon has been an invaluable guide along this path for close to twenty years.

The first time I showed up at a Healing Conference which "Pastor Sharon" was leading, I was pretty anxious. I had a whole lot of hang-ups that had kept me away from Pastor Sharon's healing ministry but the LORD kept "turning up the temperature" in my life until finally I found myself in one of her healing conferences. Here I was a trained theologian, doctrinally set against women pastors, not comfortable with expressive worship styles, etc., etc. and yet God would not give me any peace until I finally agreed to go.

At that time, I was in a really desperate place in my life where I came to realize that all the wonderful truths I "knew" about Jesus were stuck in my head and were not connected to my heart, will, and emotions. This had come as a big surprise to me—but not to my faithful partner and wife Susie. The story of how God began to pour our His Spirit into my life and emotions and heal me is a long one but suffice to say that looking back the day I met Pastor Sharon was the beginning of many of the most important experiences I have had in receiving God's grace and healing.

Pastor Sharon has become a friend and colleague through the years but so much of who I am has been tempered through my experiences at her healing schools and conferences. I have also sent literally hundreds of people to her to receive ministry in her schools and to grow and be trained to serve others as well. I have personally been to many other wonderful healing schools and have benefitted greatly, but there is something so special about the love and anointing on Pastor Sharon that she is always the standard I look to.

Part of what is so amazing about Pastor Sharon is that she combines a unique gift set that is not always found in similar ministries and Healing Schools.

- The teachings you will receive are reliable. Pastor Sharon is a gifted teacher and is a faithful expositor of God's Word. She is as solid in her thinking as she is powerful in her ministry of laying on of hands in public ministry.

- Secondly, she has developed a unique way to help people both receive ministry and grow quickly in praying effectively for others. This workbook is used in the Healing Schools that incorporate small group sessions that are invaluable to growing and learning about God's desire and willingness to heal His people.

- Perhaps the most amazing thing about Pastor Sharon's healing ministry is that she "gives it away" so beautifully! Pastor Sharon has trained up hundreds and hundreds of people in healing ministry and some of them might be leading this Healing School! The leaders she has helped grow into their own gifting and anointing are used by the LORD just as consistently to help minister and train others. This is when you know someone has really something special to offer—when they are able to help others (like you) grow into men and women whom the LORD can use to help others in their journeys.

I hope you have your seatbelt on, you are in the right place at the right time! It is such an honor for me to encourage you to open your heart as much as you can to receive from this school and grow and learn as much as I have done.

May the LORD pour out His grace healing upon you!
+Ron

The Rt. Rev'd Ron Kuykendall, Ph.D.
Sr. Pastor and Missionary Bishop
St. Andrew's Church
Gainesville, Florida

Welcome!

I and the Board of Amazing Love Healing Ministry are delighted and thrilled you are taking this Healing School Course Level One! This is the beginning of an exciting journey with God that introduces you or furthers your training in healing. Our goal is three fold:

- *Provide specific teaching in seven basic areas of healing;*
- *Provide experiences for your own healing;*
- *Provide opportunity for participating in other's healing.*

This workbook is a resource that corresponds to the Amazing Love Healing Ministry Healing School Level 1 conference series. A DVD series has also been published to go with this workbook. The best use of these materials is in conjunction with one another.

Every main teaching session begins with worship and prayer. We call upon the Holy Spirit to be present and to guide us through this healing time with the Lord. Take notes, talk with each other, listen, ask questions, meditate, reflect, worship, pray, and let the healing begin and deepen in all of us.

Many times people ask me how I got into the healing ministry. My answer is simple: I needed healing! Perhaps you too are called to this ministry to serve. Twenty-five years of experience in this ministry has confirmed for me over and over that God indeed is the God who heals us. He is our healer and longs for us to be healed to become healers in His Name on this earth. We have a saying in this ministry: wounded people wound others, but healed people through Jesus Christ heal others.

So buckle up your seat belts and let's begin!

God bless you, and may His love carry you through this beautiful journey of healing.

Love in Christ,

Rev. Dr. Sharon L. Gottfried Lewis

Amazing Love Healing Ministry

"... to bind up the broken hearted ... to give beauty for ashes ...." **Isaiah 61:1–3**

Our Vision:

A world where God's healing power is known, accepted, and shared by His people to bring healing to all!

Our Mission:

To plant healing houses/centers all over the world.

Our Venue:

- Introduction to Healing Conference
- Basic Healing Conference: "Restoring the Soul"
- Advanced Healing Conference: "Restoring the Soul"
- Eight Week Basic Healing Course: "Restoring the Soul"
- Women's Healing Conference
- Men's Healing Conference
- Marriage conference
- Private Healing Appointments
- Healing Workshops: Specific Healing Issues
- Healing Schools: Training for Healing Prayer Ministers: Levels 1, 2, 3, 4
- Lead Healing Service
- Mission Trips
- "Restoring the Soul of a Church" Conference
- Forming a Healing Ministry in Your Church
- Consulting

Executive Director: The executive director is Rev. Dr. Sharon L. Gottfried Lewis, an Episcopal priest, canonically resident in the Diocese of Southwest Florida. She holds a doctorate of ministry from Trinity School for Ministry, Ambridge, PA; Master of Divinity degree from The University of the South, Sewanee, TN; a master's degree in counseling/psychology from Nova University, Ft Lauderdale, FL, and a bachelor's degree in Education from the University of New Jersey (originally Trenton State College), Trenton,

NJ. Additional training in Christian healing modalities: Rita Bennett Basic & Advanced Healing Courses; Francis McNutt's Courses; Theophostic Training; Elijah House. Her son, Brian, and daughter-in-love, Kristy, and her precious granddaughter, Zoë, live in Maryland.

Rev. Dr. Sharon L. Gottfried Lewis

Contacting us:

Amazing Love Healing Ministry is a 501c3, nonprofit, nondenominational ministry located in Nokomis, FL.

info@amazinglovehealing.com

Subscribe to be on our mailing list at www.amazinglovehealing.com

TABLE OF CONTENTS

Chapter 1 Outline

God Heals

> **Key Concepts:**
> - **God Heals**
> - **Healing and the Triune Person**
> - **Inner Healing or Spirit/Soul Healing**
> - **Inner Child**
> - **Sources of Emotional Hurts**
> - **The Past**
> - **Blocks to Healing**

DOES GOD HEAL?

"I am the LORD, who heals you." (Exodus 15:26)

"The Spirit of the Sovereign LORD is on me, because the LORD has anointed me to preach good news to the poor. He has sent me to bind up the brokenhearted, to proclaim freedom for the captives and release from darkness for the prisoners, to proclaim the year of the LORD's favor and the day of vengeance of our God, to comfort all who mourn, and provide for those who grieve in Zion—to bestow on them a crown of beauty instead of ashes, the oil of joy instead of mourning, and a garment of praise instead of a spirit of despair. They will be called oaks of righteousness, a planting of the LORD for the display of his splendor." (Isaiah 61:1–3; Luke 4:18,)

"Jesus went throughout Galilee, teaching in their synagogues, preaching the good news of the kingdom, and healing every disease and sickness among the people." (Matthew 4:23)

"He who was seated on the throne said, 'I am making everything new!'" (Revelation 21:5a)

Healing

Healing is at the very heart of God!

HEALING AND THE TRIUNE PERSON
- We are made in God's image! (Genesis 1:26)—Father, Son, and Holy Spirit.
- We are a triune person.
  1. **BODY:** (Greek: *soma*)
  2. **SOUL:** (Greek: *psuche*) (1 Chronicles 22:19; Ps 23:3; Ps 119:75; Proverbs 6:32; Matthew 10:28; John 12:27; 3 John 2; Intellect—will—emotions (Luke 22:42) Old Testament: Hebrew: *nephesh*
  3. **SPIRIT:** (Greek: *pneuma*) (Job 32:8; Proverbs 20:27; 1 Corinthians 6:20; Ecclesiastes 12:7; Ezekiel 11: 19, 36:26; 18:31; Psalm 51:10–12)

- The **SOUL's and the SPIRIT'S** components:

INTELLECT:
EMOTIONS: (Proverbs 23:7—*"As he thinks in his heart, so is he,"* NKJV)
THE WILL:

WHAT IS INNER HEALING OR SPIRIT/SOUL HEALING?
- It is the healing of the inner self through Christ.
- Spirit/soul healing addresses the past emotional hurts and traumatic experiences in life that have left emotional pain, trauma, insecurity, and unforgiveness.

> ## Things to Remember
> - Healing begins when you accept Jesus Christ as Savior and Lord.
> - Jesus is Lord of your past, present, and future.
> - Spirit/soul healing does not change the past; it changes your perspective of the past.

"Jesus Christ is the same yesterday and today and forever." (Hebrews 13:8)

"Therefore, if anyone is in Christ, he is a new creation; the old has gone, the new has come! All this is from God, who reconciled us to himself through Christ and gave us the ministry of reconciliation: that God was reconciling the world to himself in Christ, not counting men's sins against them. And he has committed to us the message of reconciliation." (2 Corinthians 5:17–19)

WHAT IS THE INNER CHILD?
- **INNER CHILD:** It is the part of you that retains feelings and memories experienced in childhood.
- **CREATIVE CHILD:** It is the healed part of you from childhood that enables you to be creative, spontaneous, etc.
- **HURT CHILD:** It is the part of you not healed from childhood events or memories sometimes displayed in adulthood as temper tantrums, pouting, etc.

Root causes: Unhealed hurts, traumas, unforgiveness, and other healing issues have a root cause in one's past. The "fruit" of one's present behavior comes from this "root."

Mark 9:21—*"Jesus asked the boy's father, 'How long has he been like this?' 'From childhood,' he answered."*

"FOLLOW THE FRUIT TO THE ROOT"

Some examples of questions to ask for the "root cause" are:

- Have your ever felt this feeling before? When?
- How long have you believed this way?
- What made you fearful as a child?
- When were you first afraid?
- What was your first hurtful memory?
- Who did you first feel loved you?

SOURCES OF EMOTIONAL HURTS

- **UNHEALED HURTS:** Unhealed hurts are birthed in our soul when we lose something good that we had received and is required to be whole and healthy.
- **UNMET NEEDS:** Unmet needs are birthed in our soul when we did not acquire all that we needed to be whole.
- **UNRESOLVED ISSUES:** Unresolved issues are birthed in our soul when we do not know how to effectively and constructively process our unmet needs and unhealed hurts.

WHY DEAL WITH THE PAST?

a. The event occurred in the **PAST**, but the pain is experienced in the **PRESENT**.

b. Good behaviors, healthy attitudes, and physical wellness can be traced to positive childhood experiences, good upbringing, nurturing, and good physical care.

c. Negative behaviors, wrong attitudes, fears, anxiety, unforgiveness, and many physical illnesses find their root in past hurts or traumatic events, unresolved life situations, and times when our basic needs for love and nurturing were not being met.

Kinds of Inner Healing Prayer

- Healing of a memory: An inner healing prayer experience in which the person being prayed for responds to a memory that is revealed by the Holy Spirit.
- Happy memory prayer: An inner healing prayer in which the Holy Spirit brings to mind a happy memory in a person's life.
- Creative Prayer: In following the Holy Spirit's lead, the person may experience a creative event or revelation that is not an actual memory or real life event.
- Dispelling lies: In this form of inner healing prayer, the individual being prayed for expresses beliefs that have been present in specific or general life circumstances.

BLOCKS TO HEALING

a. Not accepting Jesus Christ as SAVIOR and LORD

b. Denying the power of Holy Spirit

c. Fear/Anger

d. Unconfessed Sin

e. Unforgiveness

f. Rationalization

g. Generational Sin
h. Blocked Emotions
i. Demonic Oppression
j. Strongholds
k. Denial of wounds

Barriers to Healing

Three great barriers to personal and spiritual wholeness in Christ:

- *Failure of self-acceptance*
- *Failure to forgive others*
- *Failure to receive forgiveness for oneself*

---

[1] Leanne Payne, *Restoring the Christian Soul: Overcoming Barriers to Completion in Christ through Healing Prayer* (Grand Rapids: Baker Books, 1996).

HOW DO YOU KNOW YOU NEED HEALING?

1) Having a repetitive need or a craving for too much of anything
2) Dissatisfied a lot; grass is greener somewhere else
3) Trying to fill empty places inside with things other than God
4) Overt, blatant, conscious sin in my life
5) Unforgiveness in my heart
6) Lack of freedom in relationships: with God and/or people
7) Uncomfortable with myself or others
8) Negative memories keep coming up
9) Don't get along with parents or other family members
10) Outbursts of anger, temper tantrums
11) Critical or judgmental of others, of self
12) Repeating dreams
13) Feelings of low self-worth
14) Feelings of superiority
15) Lack of freedom in worship
16) Often sarcastic
17) Lack of repentance
18) Control issues
19) Feel victimized
20) Can't express feelings easily
21) Want to get even with someone
22) Fearful
23) Self-consciousness
24) Ungodly sorrow
25) You are here!

SMALL GROUP DISCUSSION
QUESTIONS and PRAYERS
God Heals

In your small groups, please use one or more of these questions or discussion initiatives to start your group. Remember to use most of your time for prayer.

1) First introduce yourselves: who you are and why you came to this conference. Share one personal thing you would like the group to know about you.

_____

_____

_____

2) There are listed three barriers to healing. Can you identify any of these barriers in your life? If so, which one(s)?

_____

_____

_____

3) Look at the list on "How do you know you need healing?" Which one(s) apply to you?

_____

_____

_____

PRAYER TIME:
1) Affirmation Prayer
2) The 23rd Psalm

SCRIPTURAL REFERENCES

BODY
1 Corinthians 6:20—"You were bought at a price. Therefore honor God with your body."
1 Corinthians 15:44—"It is sown a natural body, it is raised a spiritual body. If there is a natural body, there is also a spiritual body."

BRIDE
Isaiah 61:10—"I delight greatly in the Lord; my soul rejoices in my God. For he has clothed me with garments of salvation and arrayed me in a robe of righteousness, as a bridegroom adorns his head like a priest, and as a bride adorns herself with her jewels."
Jeremiah 2:2—"Go and proclaim in the hearing of Jerusalem: "I remember the devotion of your youth, how as a bride you loved me and followed me through the desert, through a land not sown."
Revelation 19:7—"Let us be glad and rejoice and give Him glory, for the marriage of the Lamb has come, and His wife has made herself ready." (NKJV)

FREEDOM
2 Corinthians 3:17—"Where the spirit of the Lord is, there is freedom."

GOD LIVES IN US
1 John 4:13–15—"We know that we live in him and he in us, because he has given us of his Spirit. And we have seen and testify that the Father has sent his Son to be the Savior of the world. If anyone acknowledges that Jesus is the Son of God, God lives in him and he in God.
Romans 8:9—"You, however, are controlled not by the sinful nature but by the Spirit, if the Spirit of God lives in you. And if anyone does not have the Spirit of Christ, he does not belong to Christ."

HEALING OF MEMORIES
Isaiah 43:18–19—"Forget the former things; do not dwell on the past. See, I am doing a new thing! Now it springs up; do you not perceive it? I am making a way in the desert and streams in the wasteland."

PETER'S DENIAL OF CHRIST AND HIS RESTORATION
John 18:18—"It was cold, and the servants and officials stood around a fire they had made to keep warm. Peter also was standing with them, warming himself."
John 21:7—"Then the disciple whom Jesus loved said to Peter, 'It is the Lord!' As soon as Simon Peter heard him say, 'It is the Lord,' he wrapped his outer garment around him (for he had taken it off) and jumped into the water... When they landed, they saw a fire of burning coals there with fish on it, and some bread... When they had finished eating, Jesus said to Simon Peter, 'Simon son of John, do you truly love me more than these?' 'Yes, Lord,' he said, 'you know that I love you.' Jesus said, 'Feed my lambs.'"

HUMAN SPIRIT
Job 32:8—"But it is the spirit in a man, the breath of the Almighty that gives him understanding."
Ezekiel 11:19—"Then I will give them one heart, and I will put a new spirit within them, and take the stony heart out of their flesh, and give them a heart of flesh." (NKJV)

LOVE

John 14:23—Jesus answered and said to him, 'If anyone loves Me, he will keep My word; and My Father will love him, and We will come to him and make Our home with him.'" (NKJV)

Deuteronomy 7:13—"He will love you and bless you and increase your numbers. He will bless the fruit of your womb, the crops of your land—your grain, new wine and oil—the calves of your herds and the lambs of your flocks in the land that he swore to your forefathers to give you."

Jeremiah 31:3-6—"The Lord has appeared of old to me, saying: 'Yes, I have loved you with an everlasting love; therefore with lovingkindness I have drawn you. Again I will build you, and you shall be rebuilt, O virgin of Israel! You shall again be adorned with your tambourines, and shall go forth in the dances of those who rejoice. You shall yet plant vines on the mountains of Samaria; the planters shall plant and eat them as ordinary food. For there shall be a day when the watchmen will cry on Mount Ephraim, 'Arise, and let us go up to Zion, to the Lord our God.'" (NKJV)

Hosea 14:4—"I will heal their backsliding, I will love them freely, for my anger has turned away from him. (NKJV)

John 14:23—"Jesus answered and said to him, 'If anyone loves me, he will keep my word; and my Father will love him, and we will come to him and make our home with him.'" (NKJV)

John 15:9—"As the Father loved me, I also have loved you; abide in my love." (NKJV)

John 15:13-14—"Greater love has no one than this, than to lay down one's life for his friends. You are my friends if you do whatever I command you." (NKJV)

Romans 5:8—"But God demonstrates His own love toward us, in that while we were yet sinners, Christ died for us." (NASB)

Romans 5:5—"And hope does not disappoint us, because God has poured out his love into our hearts by the Holy Spirit, whom he has given us."

Ephesians 1:4—"Just as He chose us in Him before the foundation of the world, that we should be holy and blameless before Him." (NASB)

Ephesians 3:17-19—"So that Christ may dwell in your hearts through faith. And I pray that you, being rooted and established in love, may have power, together with all the saints, to grasp how wide and long and high and deep is the love of Christ, and to know this love that surpasses knowledge—that you may be filled to the measure of all the fullness of God."

2 Thessalonians 3:5—"And the Lord directs your hearts into the love of God, and into the patient waiting for Christ." (KJV)

MIND

Romans 12:16–"Be of the same mind toward one another. Do not set your mind on high things, but associate with the humble. Do not be wise in your own opinion." (NKJ)

1 Corinthians 2:16—"For who has known the mind of the Lord that he may instruct him? But we have the mind of Christ." (NIV)

Philippians 2:5—"Let this mind be in you which was also in Christ Jesus. . . (NKJV)

2 Timothy 1:7—"For God did not give us a spirit of timidity, but a spirit of power, of love and of self-discipline."

REBELLION

Psalm 107:10-14—"Some sat in darkness and the deepest gloom, prisoners suffering in iron chains, for they had rebelled against the words of God and despised the counsel of the Most High. So he subjected them to bitter labor; they stumbled, and there was no one to help. Then they cried to the Lord in their trouble, and he saved them from their distress. He brought them out of darkness and the deepest gloom and broke away their chains."

SATISFACTION

2 Peter 1:3—"His divine power has given us everything we need for life and godliness through our knowledge of him who called us by his own glory and goodness."

SOCIETAL HEALING

2 Chronicles 7:14—"If my people, who are called by my name, will humble themselves and pray and seek my face and turn from their wicked ways, then will I hear from heaven and will forgive their sin and will heal their land."

SOUL

Psalm 23:3—"He restores my soul; he leads me in the paths of righteousness for His name's sake." (NKJV)
Matthew 10:28—"Do not be afraid of those who kill the body but cannot kill the soul. Rather, be afraid of the One who can destroy both soul and body in hell."

SPIRITUAL HEALING

John 1:12—"Yet to all who received him, to those who believed in his name, he gave the right to become children of God."

TRINITY OF MAN

1 Thessalonians 5:23—"May God himself, the God of peace, sanctify you through and through. May your whole spirit, soul and body be kept blameless at the coming of our Lord Jesus Christ."

UNFAILING LOVE

Proverbs 20:6—"Many a man claims to have unfailing love, but a faithful man who can find?"

Psalm 100:5—"For the Lord is good and his love endures forever; his faithfulness continues through all generations."

Basics of Inner Healing Prayer

I. God Wants His People Healed
    a. Wholeness is holiness.
    b. In order for the Body of Christ to fulfill its mission, we must be healed!

II. We Are Made In God's Image
    a. We are a triune person. (1 Thessalonians 5:23)
        i. Spirit
        ii. Soul
            1. Intellect
            2. Will
            3. Emotions
        iii. Body
    b. God wants to heal our WHOLE PERSON (Gregory of Nazianzus).

III. Kinds of Healing
    a. (SPIRIT) Spiritual Healing—Personal Sin
    b. (SOUL) Emotional Healing—Past Hurts
    c. (BODY) Physical Healing—Disease or Accidents
    d. Demonic Oppression

IV. What is the INNER CHILD?
    a. Inner Child
        i. We are called to be childlike. (Matthew 19:14)
        ii. We are called to put away *childish* ways. (1 Corinthians 13:11)
    b. Creative Child
    c. Hurt Child

V. Why deal with the PAST?
    a. The event occurred in the PAST, but the PAIN is experienced in the PRESENT.
    b. Good behaviors, healthy attitudes, and physical wellness can be traced to positive childhood experiences, good upbringing, nurturing, and good physical care.
    c. Negative behaviors, wrong attitudes, fears, anxiety, unforgiveness, and many physical illnesses find their root in past hurts or traumatic events, unresolved life situations, and times when our basic needs for love and nurturing were not being met.

VI. What is INNER HEALING?
    a. "Prayer ministry that helps the Christian to become whole or holy in his or her soul. You recognize that Jesus is Lord of your past as well as your present and future. He is Lord of all!" (Rita Bennett—*Emotionally Free*)
    b. "The idea behind inner healing is simply that we can ask Jesus Christ to walk back to the time we were hurt and to free us from the effects of that wound in the present." (Francis MacNutt—*Healing*)
    c. Sources of SOUL HURTS (Liberty Savard—*Shattering Your Strongholds*)
        i. Unhealed Hurts
        ii. Unmet Needs

     iii. Unresolved Issues

  d. People who are wounded wound others. People who are healed through Jesus Christ heal others.

VII. Kinds of INNER HEALING PRAYER

  a. Healing of a Memory: An inner healing prayer in which the person being prayed for responds to a memory that is revealed by the Holy Spirit.

  b. Happy Memory Prayer: An inner healing prayer in which the Holy Spirit brings to mind a happy memory in a person's life.

  c. Creative Prayer: In following the Holy Spirit's lead, the person may experience a creative event or revelation that is not an actual memory or real-life event.

  d. Dispelling Lies: In this form of inner healing prayer, the individual being prayed for expresses beliefs that have been present in specific or general life circumstances.

VIII. What INNER HEALING IS NOT

  a. It is NOT a re-confession of past sins.

  b. It is NOT digging into the past.

  c. It is NOT teaching people to forget or deny their hurts.

  d. It is NOT giving advice or rationalization or counseling.

  e. It is NOT a psychological gimmick.

  f. It is NOT behavior modification.

  g. It is NOT simply learning to cope with the pain.

IX. Blocks to Healing

  a. Not accepting Jesus Christ as SAVIOR and LORD

  b. Denying the power of Holy Spirit

  c. Fear

  d. Unconfessed Sin

  e. Unforgiveness

  f. Rationalization

  g. Generational Sin

  h. Blocked Emotions

  i. Demonic Oppression

  j. Denial of wounds

Notes:

Chapter 2 Outline

Healing Unhealed Hurts

Key Concepts:
- **Inner Healing**
- **Inner Child**
- **Root Causes: "Fruit to Root"**
- **Kinds of Soul Healing Prayer**
- **Renouncing Past Behaviors and Practices**

<u>WHAT IS INNER HEALING? REVIEW</u>

Inner healing is the healing of the inner self and is often referred to in any of the following ways:
1) Soul Healing
2) Emotional Healing
3) Healing of Memories
4) Transformation

"Therefore, if anyone is in Christ, he is a new creation; old things have passed away; behold, all things have become new." (2 Corinthians. 5:17)

"Therefore, having been justified by faith, we have peace with God through our Lord Jesus Christ, through whom also we have access by faith into this grace in which we stand, and rejoice in hope of the glory of God." (Romans 5:1–2)

Soul healing prayer is allowing Jesus, who is NOT hampered by time, to bring healing to areas of our emotions. <u>Jesus' desire is to be Lord of our past, as well as our presents and our futures.</u>

"Jesus is the same yesterday, today, and forever." (Hebrews 13:8)

<u>Soul healing does not change the past. Soul healing changes our perspective of the past.</u> During soul healing prayer, Jesus is allowed to bring events to the surface <u>as he directs</u>. Jesus makes himself known in these past

circumstances, and brings healing through his mercy and love. *(Facilitators are not on hand to give you advice; they are on hand to help facilitate what Jesus wants to do for you and in you.)* You are not being asked to forget your past hurts, but you are being freed from the pain of them, so you can learn from them and move forward with your life.

Soul healing is helping the Christian become whole in the soul: <u>This is done not by changing the past, but by changing the influence of the past on our lives.</u>

We might refer to these negative influences in our past as:

o   Skeletons in the closet
o   Ghosts of the past
o   A reoccurring bad dream
o   The person you can't forgive
o   The embarrassing moment that is always fresh in your mind
o   The "pet peeve" that makes you fly off the handle
o   The bad feeling or impending doom feeling you just can't shake
o   The old tape that keeps running in your mind

Inner healing <u>focuses on the promises of God for you</u> and restores, proclaims and acclaims who you are, and always have been, in Christ. Inner healing dispels the lies of the enemy from your mind, will, and emotions. His truth sets you free.

INNER CHILD

<u>Definition of the inner child</u>: Rita Bennett, in *The Emotionally Free Course Basic Training*, speaks of the Inner Child as follows:

> "Your inner child or child/self is the person you were in your childhood which is a part of you today. Within the inner child is the creative child (Matt. 18:3) and the hurt child (1 Cor. 13:11). Your inner child is speaking of your emotions, which are joined to corresponding memories, stemming from your conception to your sixth (mental) year. Inner child work, in prayer, deals with freeing your adult self from world-views and self-views you may have adopted to survive as a child. It is letting Jesus take your child self by the hand and show you His unconditional love in specific ways during those early years."[2]

Rita Bennett further expounds on the Creative Child and the Hurt Child:

> "The Creative Child is made up of all the healed and healthy attitudes and memories of your early life that can help you to be: open, loving, quick to forgive, trusting, imaginative, spontaneous, creative, playful, inquisitive, unaffected, free, willing to try new things, and responsive....
>
> The Hurt Child is made up of the unhealed attitudes, memories, and reactions to those memories which sometimes cause us to regress to negative childhood behavior. The more injured a person is, the more often he will find himself feeling and acting like this Hurt Child. The childish adult at times may: throw temper tantrums to get control, pout, speak in childish whiny voice, cry

---

[2]   Rita Bennett, *The Emotionally Free Course Basic Training* (Edmonds, WA: Christian Renewal Association, Inc.,1998), pp.. 3–14.

Healing School Level 1 Workbook

to get his way, throw things, be extremely self-centered, think the world revolves around him, avoid responsibility, run away from home and problems, ... resist change, take refuge in fantasy."[3]

"And He said: 'I tell you the truth, unless you change and become like little children, you will never enter the kingdom of heaven.'" (Matthew 18:3)

"When I was a child, I talked as a child, I thought like a child, I reasoned like a child. When I became a man, I put childish ways behind me." (1 Corinthians 13:11)

ROOT CAUSES

The concept of "root causes," or "first causes," refers to the initial incident when the emotional hurt first occurred, or when the destructive lie was first believed.

Mark 9:21: "Jesus asked the boy's father, 'How long has he been like this?' 'From childhood,' he answered."

FOLLOW THE FRUIT TO THE ROOT

Example questions that may help a person ask for the "root cause" are:
- Have your ever felt this feeling before? When?
- How long have you believed this way?
- What made you fearful as a child?
- When were you first afraid?
- What was your first hurtful memory?
- Who did you first feel loved you?
- What are you feeling in your body right now?
- What is your first happy memory?

---

[3] Rita Bennett, *The Emotionally Free Course Basic Training* (Edmonds, WA: Christian Renewal Association, Inc., 2004), pp. 3-i.

KINDS OF SOUL HEALING PRAYER

Four types of inner healing (or soul healing) prayer:

A) **Healing of a memory prayer:**

An inner healing prayer experience in which the person being prayed for responds to a memory that is revealed through the Holy Spirit.

"Jesus is the same yesterday, today, and forever." (Hebrews 13:8)

"And surely I am with you always, to the very end of the age." (Matthew 28:20b)

B) **Happy memory prayer**

An inner healing prayer in which the Holy Spirit brings to mind a happy memory in a person's life.

C) **Creative prayer**

In following the Holy Spirit's lead, the person may experience a creative event or revelation that is not an actual memory or real-life event. The person may even be brought experientially through a parable or Bible story in the Bible by the Holy Spirit.

"'For My thoughts are not your thoughts, neither are your ways my ways,' declares the Lord. 'As the heavens are higher than the earth, so are my ways higher than your ways and my thoughts than your thoughts.'" (Isaiah. 55:8–9)

D) **Dispelling Lies**

In this form of inner healing prayer, the individual being prayed for expresses beliefs that have been present in specific or general life circumstances that are not true. The Holy Spirit will dispel the lies and bring the truth to every situation in the person's life.

"Then you will know the truth, and the truth will set you free." (John 8:32)

RENOUNCING PAST BEHAVIORS AND PRACTICES

Behaviors, beliefs, or ritualistic practices that he/she has been involved with that continue to have a "negative hold" on one's life.

- Renounced: Willfully act to give up, abandon, or disown a spirit or behavior that does not bring glory to God.
- Renouncing: An open declaration or proclamation of one's intent.
- Renouncing is done "in the Name of Jesus" and by His authority by the person who is receiving prayer.
- Forgiveness is asked of the Lord for participating in the behavior or false belief.
- Prayer facilitators pray that the Holy Spirit fill and dwell in all places in the individual that have been "emptied" through the renouncing prayer.

Examples of bondages (past negative behaviors, patterns, or wrong choices) are:
- **Cults**: Any belief that is not a Judeo-Christian belief. Instead, it teaches that there is some other way to heaven than through Jesus Christ and does not profess or confess Jesus Christ as the Son of God. (See Micah 4:5 and 1 John 4:1–2)
- **Occults:** Pertains to magic, astrology, and other alleged sciences, or groups that practice these sciences, claiming to seek, manipulate, or use information obtained from the spiritual world for their own purposes that are often evil. (See Deuteronomy. 18:9–14; Acts 19:19)

- **Sexual Involvement**: Inappropriate, illicit involvement in sexual activity outside of marriage; perverted or deviant sexual activities; pornography, unbiblical sexual behavior. (See Leviticus 18; 1 Corinthians 6:18; Romans 1:26–32)
- **Addictions**: Compulsive dependence on drugs, alcohol, relationships, gambling, or other behaviors that take precedence in our lives, removing God from His rightful place in us; idolatry. (See Romans 1:25; 7:14–25; 1 Corinthians 6:19)

Specific information on these four areas of bondage can be found on the *Checklist for Areas of Bondage* in the prayer chapter of this notebook, followed by a *Prayer of Renouncing*, which will be taught in the *Authority and Spiritual Warfare* teaching.

SUMMARY:

We are called to be healers and reconcilers with Jesus Christ. It begins with our own healing first and then goes forth to others!

SMALL GROUP DISCUSSION
QUESTIONS and PRAYERS
Healing Unhealed Hurts

1) What came to your mind about your own childhood during the teaching about the Inner Child? Were you a Creative Child or a Hurt Child?

    _____

    _____

    _____

2) What needs were met for you as a child? By whom? What needs did not seem to be met for you?

    _____

    _____

    _____

3) Has the Holy Spirit ever reminded you of a related past memory or event when you were struggling with a current situation? What did you do with it at that time? Would you like to share it now?

    _____

    _____

    _____

Prayer Experience: Inner Healing Prayer

APPENDIX AND SCRIPTURES

Putting on the Armor of God—Ephesians 6:13–18

Lord, I gratefully put on the armor you provided for me, that I might be ready to do your will.

I put on the **Helmet of Salvation**—it covers my mind, thoughts, and what I dwell on. Casting down every vain imagination that exalts itself against you, I bring every thought captive to the Lord Jesus Christ. For your Word says "I have the mind of Christ."

It covers my eyes, what I see, look at, and perceive. Your Word says, "If the eye be single the whole body be full of light," and my eyes are singly on you, Lord.

It covers my ears, what I hear, listen to, and understand. Your Word says, "My sheep hear my voice and no other will they follow."

It covers my nose. I can smell the sweet fragrance of your presence, Lord, The Rose of Sharon and The Lilly of the Valley. I can also smell the evil, horrid, sulfurous odor of Satan.

It covers my mouth, what I speak, declare, and proclaim. Your Word says, "Life and death are in the tongue," and I choose life.

It also covers my neck, which is not stiff and arrogant or rebellious toward you, but yielded and humble.

Thank you, Lord, for your Helmet of Salvation, the Precious Blood of Jesus. It covers every entrance place into me.

I put on the **Breastplate of Righteousness**. It covers my filthiness with your Righteousness, and brings me into right standing with God the Father. It keeps my emotions in balance with Jesus, and covers my heart that is deceitful above all things. I ask you to "Search me, Oh God, and know my heart, try me and know my thoughts, and see if there be any wickedness in me, and lead me in the Way everlasting." Create in me a clean heart, Oh God, and renew in me a right spirit. Cast me not from Thy presence and take not the Holy Spirit from me." I want to have clean hands and a pure heart that I might come before you.

I put on the **Belt of Truth** around my loins, my birthing place, my mind, where I think, my mouth, where I speak, my heart, where the issues of life are, and my emotions, where I feel, so that I am girded about in truth. For if you know the Truth, the Truth will set you free.

I put on the **Shoes of the Gospel of Peace** that I might be ready to do your will; to go to the left, to the right, straight ahead or turn around: to stand still, walk, or run at your command. I will take back the territory the enemy has stolen and bring the Gospel of Peace, Love, and Forgiveness to all you put in my path.

I take up the **Shield of Faith** to ward off the fiery darts of the enemy. Grow my faith in you and perfect and complete that faith to your honor and glory.

I take up the **Sword of the Spirit**, which is the Word of God. It is sharper than any two-edged sword, to reveal first the motivations, intents and purposes of my heart and then wherever you send it; to pierce the darkness, cut off evil, or prune for more fruit. Guide my hand, Lord, with your hand.

Thank you for the ability to **pray in the Spirit at all times**, to praise and worship you, to intercede or be in fellowship with you.

Over all, I put on the mantle of Love and the mantle of Humility, that all might be done in your perfect justice. Amen.

Notes:

Chapter 3 Outline

Closed Doors To Healing—Part 1

Key Concepts:
- **In Need of Salvation**
- **Denial—Am I Willing?**
- **Inner Vows**
- **Word Curses**

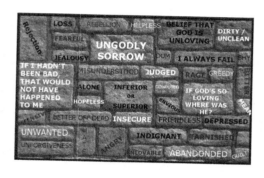

I)   IN NEED OF SALVATION

GOD IS LOVE. Love, by its very nature, seeks expression.

God created Adam and Eve to receive His love and walk in fellowship with Him. God loved Adam and Eve, enough to give them the choice to love Him back or not to return His love.

In the Garden of Eden, they had to face that choice. Their obedience to God was a confirmation of their love for God. Their disobedience was a confirmation of their love of self. Love involves trust. When we don't trust God, we have not received His love fully nor can we love Him fully.

Satan's (known as Lucifer) challenge to Adam and Eve came in a subtle appeal to their **SOULS** (Genesis 3:1-6):

- To their **MINDS** (intellect)
- Their **WILLS**
- Their **EMOTIONS**

SATAN DID NOT APPEAL TO THEIR SPIRIT BECAUSE HE KNEW THAT THEIR SPIRITS BELONGED FULLY TO GOD

Why does Satan tempt us? Temptation is Satan's invitation to give in to his kind of life and give up on God's kind of life (Genesis 3:1–6). **We must realize being tempted is not a sin.** We have not sinned until we give in to the temptation.

SALVATION: DO YOU HAVE A PERSONAL RELATIONSHIP WITH JESUS CHRIST?

> John 3:3-8 "Jesus answered him, I assure you, most solemnly I tell you, that unless a person is born again (anew, from above), he cannot ever see (know, be acquainted with, and experience) the kingdom of God. Nicodemus said to Him, How can a man be born when he is old? Can he enter his mother's womb again and be born? Jesus answered, I assure you, most solemnly I tell you, unless a man is born of water and [even] the Spirit, he cannot [ever] enter the kingdom of God. What is born of [from] the flesh is flesh [of the physical is physical]; and what is born of the Spirit is spirit." (Amplified Bible)

How do we receive or experience salvation?

> Romans 10:9, 10, 13 "Because if you acknowledge and confess with your lips that Jesus is Lord and in your heart believe (adhere to, trust in, and rely on the truth) that God raised Him from the dead, you will be saved. . . For with the heart a person believes (adheres to, trusts in, and relies on Christ) and so is justified (declared righteous, acceptable to God), and with the mouth he confesses (declares openly and speaks out freely his faith) and confirms [his] salvation. . . For everyone who calls upon the name of the Lord [invoking Him as Lord] will be saved." (Amplified Bible)

Jesus Christ atoned for all the sins of the world on the cross. He made the way for each person to have salvation. However, accepting salvation is a choice each person has to make for oneself.

Repentance is not an emotion, it is an action.

There are different things that can block us in healing prayer: Unforgiveness from the will; the scene is too hard; healing is needed from the Father; angry at God, the hurt is too fresh; bondage from cults and occults; needs practice seeing by Faith; doesn't think God can heal them, generational sin; deliverance needed.

Forgiveness is a choice. Learning to walk out our new way of life often requires us to correct wrong life's patterns. A block to healing is anything that stands in the way of God healing us or of us becoming all He created us to become. We must allow Him to transform our stinking thinking, our habits of putting our desires above His. Through Jesus healing us, we begin thinking with the mind of Christ.

What forgiveness is not: condoning, excusing, denying an offence; does not imply trust or trust-worthiness; is not the same as reconciliation.

One major block: "I must overcome the issue before Christ can love and accept me." Our efforts can never determine the love of Christ. He hates the sin but loves the sinner.

II) DENIAL: Denial—the action of declaring something to be untrue.
We allow denial to build strongholds, which we express in different ways:

- Unconfessed sin
- Unforgiveness—Jesus, others, you (robs you of JOY)
- Rationalization
- Failure of self-acceptance

What is a stronghold? A stronghold is a place that has been fortified so as to protect it against attack. It is a place where a particular cause or believe is strongly defended or upheld whether it is right or not.

Strongholds occur because
1. We are human and not perfect. Only Christ is perfect. Wounding and events in our lives have taught us how to react to life.
2. We live in denial.

   - "I don't have any problems." (I don't recognize them as a problem.)
   - Minimizing: "Oh, it's really not as bad as it sounds." So you don't even accept it is as issue at all. "Just dabbling with sin a little doesn't mean I have an issue in that area. I'm just messing around." Satan will try to convince you that sinning in little ways is acceptable.
   - Worse yet, **total denial**. Not accepting a problem exists at all.
   - Fear of failure, even fear of success.
   - Blame shifting: "I only hit her once, doesn't mean I have an anger issue, I didn't mean to give her a black eye. If she had not said those things to me, I would have walked away. She wanted me to fight him. Adam blamed God: "It was that woman you gave me."

II)   INNER VOWS:

An inner vow is a determination that is set by the mind and heart earl in life. Vows we make today also affect us. Inner vows we make as children are established in us and are usually forgotten. Our inner being retains such programming no matter what changes our heart and mind later. You can tell you have an inner vow at work within you because it resists the normal maturation process. Inner vows resist change and we do not grow out of them. Only through Jesus Christ are they exposed, healed, and broken.

Inner vows often begin with, "I will never. . .," or "I will always. . ."

- I will never be like my dad (or mom).

- I will always take care of myself.

- I will never grow up.

- I'll always be a failure, no matter how hard I try; I'll mess things up!

- I'll never let anyone get close to me again.

   A. Breaking an inner vow:

      1. <u>Recognition:</u> If you don't remember the inner vow in your conscience mind the Holy Spirit will reveal it if you ask.
      2. <u>Forgiveness:</u> Explore and begin the process of forgiving those who have hurt you and yourself. Ask forgiveness of God for judging and taking on his job of judge.

3. <u>Confess and repent</u> of sinful actions which led to the making of the vow.

4. <u>Renounce the vow:</u> Vows can be broken by the authority given us by Jesus Christ. Use the authority of binding and loosing (Matthew 16:19, 18:18). You may also be led by the Holy Spirit to speak to an inner child part of you that needs to be released from the vow.

5. Healing of memories is usually needed when dealing with inner vows.

6. Tell the Lord you are <u>ready and willing to accept the gifts</u> He has been waiting to give you (or the one prayed with).

7. <u>Persevere:</u> We must overcome long practiced habits.

III) WORD CURSES (THE POWER OF WORDS ARE LIFE AND DEATH)

In Matthew 12:33–39, Jesus talks about good fruit comes from good trees, and bad fruit from bad trees. Out from our heart flows what is stored up in us. What we say reveals what is in our heart. What kind of words come from your mouth? You can't solve your heart problems just by cleaning up your speech. You must allow the Holy Spirit to fill you with new attitudes and motives; then your speech will be cleansed at its source. We must stop murdering our soul by the negative words we speak against our self. We must have a heart transplant that lines up with who God says we are. Even words such as "you are just like your dad" can be word curses.

Word curses often come out of our mouth with good intention. However word curses speak judgment against ourselves or others.

Principle of sowing and reaping: You sow what you will reap.

Honor the position/office of mother and father. "Honor your father and mother, as the Lord your God has commanded you, so that you may live long and that it may go well with you in the land the Lord is giving you." (Deuteronomy 5:16). You honor the position not the negative behavior.

A. Effect of Word Curses:

1. Word curses have no expiration date. Once spoken and accepted into an unsurrendered soul, these curses take on power and authority within the life of the believer.

2. Word curses become the "filter" through which the individual processes life experience. The curses are compounded by the lies of the enemy who will then use these lies to reinforce the curse.

3. Word curses may be about anything: finances, health, raising children, relationships, and expected outcomes.

B. Breaking the Power of Word Curses:

1. Identify the word curses made against us by others or ourselves. Learn to recognize when a negative forecast is being made, either by you or by another.

2. Take authority over the curse in the power and authority of Jesus Christ through the Holy Spirit who resides in us.

3. Bind yourself to Christ and to His promises for our lives. Bind yourself to the truth of His Word (pray specific Scripture verses pertinent to the area of life affected by the curse). Renounce and loose the curse off your life, loosing all the negative effects and the subsequent wrong behaviors, ideas, and beliefs that may have developed. Usually inner healing of the memories associated

with the word curse is needed. Through the Holy Spirit, Jesus speaks His truth to you, breaking the curse over you.

4. Through the blood of Jesus, ask God to forgive us for making or accepting the word curse. We forgive the others involved and we forgive ourselves.

5. We claim the power of the Holy Spirit as we covenant to walk in victory over the curse.

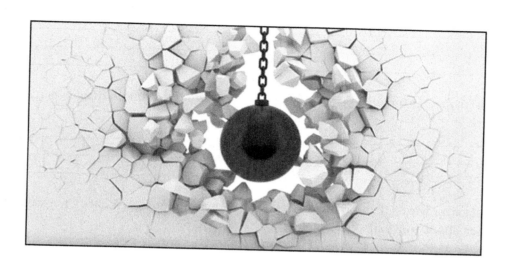

SMALL GROUP DISCUSSION
QUESTIONS and PRAYERS
Closed Doors to Healing—Part I

In your small groups, please use one or more of these questions or discussion initiatives to start your group. Remember to use most of the group time for prayer.

1) Have you yielded your will to Jesus Christ as Savior and Lord of your life?

_____

_____

_____

2) Do you participate in a denial system? What kinds of things do you do to keep pain away (addictions, activity, etc.)?

_____

_____

_____

3) Identify negative words that have been spoken by others about you. Identify negative words that you have spoken about yourself.

_____

_____

_____

4) Are you aware of any inner vow you have made concerning your parents or other authority figures in your life? Do you see evidence of the negative effects of these vows in your present life?

_____

_____

_____

SCRIPTURAL REFERENCES

Deuteronomy 28:1–2—"If you fully obey the Lord your God and carefully follow all his commands I give you today, the Lord your God will set you high above all the nations on earth. All these blessings will come upon you and accompany you if you obey the Lord your God."

Romans 2:4—"Or do you show contempt for the riches of his kindness, tolerance and patience, not realizing that God's kindness leads you toward repentance?"

Ephesians 4:15–16—"Instead, speaking the truth in love, we will in all things grow up into him who is the Head, that is, Christ. From him the whole body, joined and held together by every supporting ligament, grows and builds itself up in love, as each part does its work."

Matthew 7:17–18—"Likewise every good tree bears good fruit, but a bad tree bears bad fruit. A good tree cannot bear bad fruit, and a bad tree cannot bear good fruit."

Galatians 5:19–21—"The acts of the sinful nature are obvious: sexual immorality, impurity and debauchery; idolatry and witchcraft; hatred, discord, jealousy, fits of rage, selfish ambition, dissensions, factions and envy; drunkenness, orgies, and the like. I warn you, as I did before, that those who live like this will not inherit the kingdom of God."

Deuteronomy 5:16—"Honor your father and your mother, as the Lord your God has commanded you, so that you may live long and that it may go well with you in the land the Lord your God is giving you."

Galatians 6:7—"Do not be deceived: God cannot be mocked. A man reaps what he sows."

Matthew 16:19—"I will give you the keys of the kingdom of heaven; whatever you bind on earth will be bound in heaven, and whatever you loose on earth will be loosed in heaven."

Matthew 18:18—"I tell you the truth, whatever you bind on earth will be bound in heaven, and whatever you loose on earth will be loosed in heaven."

1 John 4:1–2—"Dear friends, do not believe every spirit, but test the spirits to see whether they are from God, because many false prophets have gone out into the world. This is how you can recognize the Spirit of God: Every spirit that acknowledges that Jesus Christ has come in the flesh is from God. . ."

Deuteronomy 18:10–13—"Let no one be found among you who sacrifices his son or daughter in the fire, who practices divination or sorcery, interprets omens, engages in witchcraft, or casts spells, or who is a medium or spiritist or who consults the dead. Anyone who does these things is detestable to the Lord, and because of these detestable practices the Lord your God will drive out those nations before you. You must be blameless before the Lord your God.

James 1:13–15—"When tempted, no one should say, 'God is tempting me.' For God cannot be tempted by evil, nor does he tempt anyone; but each one is tempted when, by his own evil desire, he is dragged away and enticed. Then, after desire has conceived, it gives birth to sin; and sin, when it is full-grown, gives birth to death."

SALVATION

"In the beginning was the Word and the Word was with God, and the Word was God. He was with God in the beginning." (John 1:1–2)

"In the beginning God created the heavens and the earth. Now the earth was formless and empty, darkness was over the surface of the deep, and the Spirit of God was hovering over the waters." (Genesis 1:1–2)

"Then God said, 'Let us make man in our image, in our likeness.' . . . so God created man in his own image, in the image of God He created him, male and female He created them." (Genesis 1:26a, 27)

"And the Lord God commanded the man, 'You are free to eat from any tree in the garden; but you must not eat from the tree of the knowledge of good and evil, for when you eat of it you will surely die.'" (Genesis 2:16)

"Then the eyes of both were opened, and they realized they were naked; so they sewed fig leaves together and made coverings for themselves." (Genesis 3:7)

"For God so loved the world that He gave His one and only Son, that whoever believes in Him shall not perish but have eternal life." (John 3:16)

"For all have sinned and fall short of the glory of God, and are justified freely by His grace through the redemption that came by Christ Jesus. God presented Him as a sacrifice of atonement through faith in His blood." (Romans 3:23–25a)

"For the wages of sin is death, but the gift of God is eternal life in Christ Jesus our Lord. (Romans 6:23)

"For Christ's love compels us, because we are convinced that One died for all, and therefore all died." (2 Corinthians 5:14)

"Let us fix our eyes on Jesus, the author and perfecter of our faith, who for the joy set before Him, endured the cross, scorning its shame, and sat down at the right hand of the throne of God." (Hebrews 12:2)

"'Abba, Father,' He said, 'Everything is possible for you. Take this cup from me. Yet not what I will, but what you will.'" (Mark 14:36)

"It is by the name of Jesus Christ of Nazareth, whom you crucified but whom God raised from the dead that this man stands before you healed... Salvation is found in no one else, for there is no other name under heaven given to men by which we must be saved." (Acts 4:10b, 12)

"I came that they may have life, and have it abundantly." (John 10:10, NASB)

"I am the way, the truth, and the life; no one comes to the Father but through me." (John 14:6, NASB)

"The word is near you; it is in your mouth and in your heart, that is, the word of faith we are proclaiming: That, if you confess with your mouth, 'Jesus is Lord,' and believe in your heart that God raised Him from the dead, you will be saved." (Romans 10:8–9)

"Anyone who trusts in Him will never be put to shame." (Romans 10:11)

"But He was pierced for our transgressions, He was crushed for our iniquities; the punishment that brought us peace was upon Him, and by His wounds we are healed." (Isaiah 53:5)

"Therefore, if anyone is in Christ, he is a new creation; the old has gone, the new has come! All this is from God, who reconciled us to Himself through Christ and gave us the ministry of reconciliation: that God was reconciling the world to Himself in Christ, not counting men's sins against them. And He has committed to us the message of reconciliation. We are therefore Christ's ambassadors, as though God was making His appeal through us. Be reconciled to God." (2 Corinthians 5:17–21)

"But you received the Spirit of sonship. And by him we cry, 'Abba, Father.' The Spirit himself testifies with our spirit that we are God's children. Now if we are children, then we are heirs— heirs of God and co-heirs with Christ, if indeed we share in His suffering in order that we may also share in His glory." (Romans 8:16–17)

"We love because He first loved us." (1 John 4:19)

"A new command I give you: Love one another. As I have loved you, so you must love one another. By this all men will know that you are my disciples, if you love one another." (John 13:34–35)

"Peace I leave with you; my peace I give you." (John 14:27a)

"If a man remains in me and I in him, he will bear much fruit; apart from Me you can do nothing. . . This is My Father's glory, that you bear much fruit, showing yourselves to be My disciples." (John 15:5, 8)

"When the Counselor comes, whom I will send to you from the Father, the Spirit of truth who goes out from the Father, He will testify about me. And you also must testify, for you have been with me from the beginning." (John 16:26–27)

"But the fruit of the Spirit is love, joy, peace, patience, kindness, goodness, faithfulness, gentleness, and self-control. . . Since we live by the Spirit, let us keep in step with the Spirit." (Galatians 5:22–23, 25)

"I tell you the truth, anyone who has faith in me will do what I have been doing. He will do even greater things than these, because I am going to the Father. And I will do whatever you ask in my name, so that the Son may bring glory to the Father." (John 14:12–13)

"For in Him, we live and move and have our being." (Acts 17:28)

"Jesus replied, 'Love the Lord your God with all your heart and with all your soul and with all your mind.' This is the first and greatest commandment. And the second is like it: 'Love your neighbor as yourself.' All the Law and the Prophets hang on these two commandments." (Matthew 22:37–40)

Notes:

Closed Doors To Healing Part II

> **Key Concepts:**
> - **Lies vs. Truth**
> - **Strongholds**
> - **Generational Bondages & Strongholds**
> - **Wrong Sexual & Psychological Soul Ties**
> - **Mind Renewal**

Introduction

Presenting problem: Situation, behavior, and/or strong, negative emotion(s) that is being experienced at the present time.

We are saved but not yet perfected. We all struggle within our souls, which is our mind, will, and emotions. The Christian's soul must be renewed through the Holy Spirit when she/he is born again. (See Romans 12:2 and Ephesians 4:22.)

Victory is possible through Christ over intense negative emotions that are creating pain. Emotions are the result of thoughts, beliefs, and interpretations of situations in our lives. When thoughts, beliefs, and interpretations are based on lies that were planted from earlier negative experiences, messages, and traumatic events, the feelings are also negative and the behavior unhealthy.

Dr. Ed Smith in *Beyond Tolerable Recovery* states that the wounds from the past are encoded in the brain through visual, emotional, and physical/sensory memories. If your parents called you stupid or worthless as a child, you may have believed that because your abstract reasoning was not developed enough to refute an authority figure's opinion of you. This lie is like a computer chip deeply embedded in your mind and is played again and again through other negative events. This negative thought keeps repeating UNTIL you come to an spiritual understanding of who you are in Christ.

WHAT STOPS US FROM COMING TO AN UNDERSTANDING OF WHO WE ARE IN CHRIST AND FROM WALKING IN FREEDOM?

Biblical Terms
    I.   Lies we have believed
    II. Strongholds
    III. Generational bondages
    IV. Wrong sexual and psychological soul ties
    V. Lack of mind renewal

Psychological terms
    I.   Irrational thoughts/Childhood messages
    II. Self-defeating patterns
    III. Family of origin dysfunctions
    IV. Codependency
    V. Need for rational and logical thoughts

We will concentrate on biblical terms because the Great Physician is God, and the Counselor is Holy Spirit. Although the "presenting problem" is usually worded by people as a "soul" problem or a "psychological" problem, the solution is spiritual!

LIES

These lies cause a person to feel fearful, abandoned, shamed, tainted, powerless, anxious, hopeless, invalidated, and confused. The emotions can be triggered in the present, but they are *rooted* in negative past events. Look for the "historical memory event" that feels the same or matches the current emotions. In the search for these lies or origin of core false beliefs, it is crucial that we are led by the Holy Spirit who will guide us into all truth.

STRONGHOLDS

"A stronghold is what one uses to fortify and defend a personal belief, idea, or opinion against outside opposition." (A paraphrase from *Thayer's Greek-English Lexicon*)

Strongholds protect wrong beliefs, attitudes, and patterns that we have learned to trust. In the beginning they may have been a survival tactic, but if left in place they will provide access for the enemy's assaults and block healing. We have learned to trust them more than we trust "the truth." Therefore, they must be demolished to allow room for the truth to set us free.

Some strongholds we build are as follows: (Information gleaned from Liberty Savard's book *Shattering Your Strongholds*).

- **Suspicion:** Being painfully deceived can cause the building of a stronghold of suspicion to protect being deceived again. This stronghold will resist intimacy with God.
- **Doubt:** The stronghold of doubt is usually one of the most obvious ones. It frequently accompanies a stronghold of suspicion, which can masquerade it so well. Its existence is often totally denied.
- **Independence:** Rejection can cause the building of a stronghold of independence and self-sufficiency around pain, fortifying a right to never be vulnerable again. This can include any vulnerability to the work of the Holy Spirit.
- **False Security:** When unmet needs exist, a stronghold of false security may be erected. This projects a cover-up of great strength intended to keep others from knowing how internally fragile and needy a person is. This can extend to keeping God at arm's length, as well.

- **Unforgiveness:** When someone has been abused or deeply hurt, unless forgiveness and healing come, strongholds of unforgiveness, bitterness, or anger are erected to justify the role of being a victim.
- **Control and Manipulation:** A childhood filled with chaos, instability, confusion, and everything seemingly out of control can build a stronghold of control to prevent ever being at the mercy of another again.
- **Self-Indulgence:** This stronghold is built to justify and protect the right to indulge self to compensate for unmet needs and pain in their past and/or present life. It also justifies a right to chemically alter reality with drugs, alcohol, or addictions, such as gambling, shopping, or work, to blot out pain.
- **Fear:** People generally do not build this stronghold for protection; rather it is erected around great apprehension and anxiety over unresolved memories and experiences.

One of the strongest strongholds is **DENIAL.** Denial can refuse to acknowledge any of the above things listed above. (See Steps to Renouncing Strongholds, appendix end of chapter 4.)

GENERATIONAL BONDAGES

Generational bondages are characteristics or patterns that are passed down from one generation to another until there is a release of the stronghold by the Word of God.

Generational strongholds can be:

A) **Physical**: cancer, diabetes, high blood pressure, etc.
B) **Emotional**: depression, fear, anxiety, anger, etc.
C) **Attitudinal**: racism, prejudices, negative self-image, self-hatred
D) **Spiritual**: lust, sexual perversion, codependent soul ties, religious spirit, spiritual abuse, etc.

(See Exodus 20:5a–6)

WRONG SEXUAL AND PSYCHOLOGICAL SOUL TIES

Sin is wrong behavior. We sin in our thoughts, in our words, and in our deeds. Wrong behaviors occur in every Christian for *"all have sinned and fall short of the glory of God"* (Romans 3:23).

Temptations of the flesh. The decision to give into the temptations of our flesh and to sin *rests with us* (see James 1:14–16).

Sin separates us from God—not from His love, but from fully (spirit, soul, and body) being in His presence. God and sin cannot reside in the same space. Sin contradicts the very nature of God.

One wrong behavior is sexual sin. Any sexual act outside of marriage is sin. Fornication, adultery, homosexuality, pornography, and sodomy are all sexual sins and are wrong in God's sight. They create wrong soul ties. You are wrongly united to that person (see 1 Corinthians 6:15–20).

Another wrong behavior is psychological soul ties. Types of these wrong soul ties include:

A) Codependent relationships
B) Possessive, controlling relationships
C) Occult relationships
D) Spiritual adulterous relationships (with someone or something other than spouse or God)

We need to confess, repent, and break any wrong ties. (See Prayer for Breaking Wrong Soul Ties Chapter 8.) Inner healing of memories is needed as well as healing the early imprinting of sexual experiences or encounters outside of marriage.

Imprinting: Impressed or stamped firmly in ones mind; to impress on one's mind to recognize something as a place of trust, etc "The two shall be one" is intended by God to be fulfilled in marriage under God's protection. As husband and wife the first sexual intimacy is imprinted in their minds and hearts forever. They can only satisfy one another. When sexual encounters occur outside of marriage this principle is still at work but now the imprinting is with someone else other than your spouse. This imprinting also occurs with viewing pornographic material.

RENEWING OF THE MIND

"Do not conform to the pattern of this world, but be transformed by the renewing of your mind. Then you will be able to test and approve what God's will is—His good, pleasing and perfect will. (Romans 12:2)

**SMALL GROUP DISCUSSION
QUESTIONS and PRAYERS
Closed Doors to Healing—Part II**

In your small groups, please use one or more of these questions or **discussion initiatives** to start your group. Remember to use most of the group time for prayer.

1) What strongholds do you identify with?

2) Looking at the Painful Memories Emotion Wall picture, which ones do you identify with?

3) Have you experienced a sexual or psychological soul tie that is continuing to affect you negatively?

4) How can we renew the mind from a "me-first" to a "God-first" mindset?

APPENDIX: PRAYERS

(1) **Prayer for breaking wrong soul ties**

Lord, I confess I have sinned against you and my body and/or soul. I have misused my body and/or soul with_____. I repent and am truly sorry for my wrongdoing. Please forgive me, Lord, and with your help, I will sin no more.

I now take the sword of the Spirit and cut each wrong spiritual, physical, mental, and emotional ties between each person with whom I have been wrongfully involved. I seal the ends with the blood of Jesus so they can never be rejoined. Thank you, Lord, that these ties no longer have any power over me. I am free in Jesus' name.

(2) **Prayer for stripping your old nature**

(Adapted from book *Shattering Your Strongholds* by Liberty Savard)

In the name of Jesus Christ, I bind my body, soul, and spirit to the will and purposes of God. I bind myself to the truth of God.

Lord, I repent of having wrong attitudes and thoughts. I renounce them and ask for your forgiveness. I loose every old, wrong pattern of thinking, attitude, idea, desire, belief, habit, and behavior that may still be working in me. I tear down, crush, smash, and destroy every stronghold I have erected to protect them.

I bind myself to the attitudes and patterns of Jesus Christ. I bind myself to the overcoming behavior and spiritual desires that line up with the fruit of the Holy Spirit.

Father, I loose any stronghold in my life protecting wrong feelings I have against anyone. Forgive me as I forgive those who have caused me pain, loss, or grief. I loose any desire for retribution or redress. In the name of Jesus, I loose the power and the effects of any harsh or hard words spoken about me, to me, or by me. I loose any strongholds connected with them. I loose all generational bondages and their strongholds from myself. Thank you, Jesus, that you have promised whatsoever I bind and loose on earth will be bound and loosed in heaven. Amen.

STEPS TO RENOUNCING STRONGHOLDS

To renounce generational sins and other strongholds:

1) Identify the stronghold, sin, or bondage pattern.
2) Renounce (give up, disown) the stronghold in the name of Jesus and by His authority claim that it has no more power over your life.
3) Claim the blood of Jesus (the work of the cross) over your present situation and back through the generations, and forward over all generations.
4) Ask the Lord's forgiveness for your own participation in the specific generational sin or tie.
5) Bind your mind, will, and emotions to Jesus Christ and His purposes for you, specifically claiming victory to walk free of the specific generational sin or tie.
6) Be accountable to another Christian for "walking out the victory."

NOTE: THERE IS A POSITIVE DEFINITION OF STRONGHOLD IN THE BIBLE AS "THE PRESENCE OF GOD." (SEE PSALM 9:9–10)

SCRIPTURAL REFERENCES

Romans 12:2–"Do not conform any longer to the pattern of this world, but be transformed by the renewing of your mind. Then you will be able to test and approve what God's will is—his good, pleasing and perfect will."

Ephesians 4:22–"You were taught, with regard to your former way of life, to put off your old self, which is being corrupted by its deceitful desires."

Exodus 20:5a–6 (MSG)—"I am God, your God, and I'm a most jealous God, punishing the children for any sins their parents pass on to them to the third and fourth generation of those who hate me. But I'm unswervingly loyal to the thousands who love me and keep my commandments."

James 1:14–16 (MSG)—"Don't let anyone under pressure to give in to evil say, "God is trying to trip me up." God is impervious to evil, and puts evil in no one's way. The temptation to give in to evil comes from us and only us. We lust. Lust gets pregnant, and has a baby: sin! Sin grows up to adulthood and becomes a real killer.

I Corinthians 6:15–20–"Do you not know that your bodies are members of Christ himself? Shall I then take the members of Christ and unite them with a prostitute? Never! Do you not know that he who unites himself with a prostitute is one with her in body? For it is said, 'The two will become one flesh.' But he who unites himself with the Lord is one with him in spirit. Flee from sexual immorality. All other sins a man commits are outside his body. Do you not know that your body is a temple of the Holy Spirit, who is in you, whom you have received from God? You are not your own; you were bought at a price. Therefore, honor God with your body."

Notes:

Chapter 5 Outline

Forgiveness

> **Key Concepts:**
> - **Components of Forgiveness: Restoring Unity**
> - **Unforgiveness: Bondage, Deception, Obstacles, High Cost**
> - **Principle of Sowing & Reaping**
> - **Keys of the Kingdom: Binding & Loosing**
> - **The Forgiveness Process**
> - **Walking in Freedom**

I) <u>COMPONENTS OF FORGIVENESS:</u>

A) RESTORING UNITY

Forgiveness is what brings us back into relationship with God and makes it possible for us to walk in unity with one another.

B) FORGIVENESS IS A CHOICE

We choose to forgive. Scripture makes this very clear. God will not force us to forgive others, but He makes the stakes of unforgiveness very high.

"For if you forgive men when they sin against you, your heavenly Father will also forgive you. But if you do not forgive men their sins, your Father will not forgive your sins." (Matthew 6:14–15)

Unforgiveness is essentially a *refusal to forgive*. We have been offended in some way.

The Father's love for us is unconditional (Lamentations 3:22–23), but His forgiveness is conditional (Matthew 6:14–15).

C) FORGIVENSS IS OUR CALLING

We are **called to live as forgiven and forgiving children** and that is radically inclusive. (John 13:34–35; Luke 6:35).

II) UNFORGIVENESS:

(1) The Bondage

Unforgiveness is essentially a lack of love.

"Unforgiveness is like dirt or filth on our inner man." (Joyce Myers, Life in the Word, June 11, 2002, TV)

(2) The Deception

We believe that by not forgiving someone, we are punishing that person. The truth is that we are the ones wounded by the unforgiveness.

(3) The Obstacles

Pride, judgment, anger, etc.

(4) The Cost

You will continue to be emotionally tied to the hurt of the past, until you forgive. You will play it over and over again in your mind. You are held in bondage. Unforgiveness is like drinking poison expecting the other person to die.

III) PRINCIPLE OF SOWING AND REAPING

An absolute law of God is the principle of sowing and reaping.

"Do not be deceived, God is not mocked; for whatever a man sows, this he will also reap." (Galatians 6:7)

IV) KEYS OF THE KINGDOM

"I will give you the keys of the kingdom of heaven; whatever you bind on earth will be bound in heaven and whatever you loose on earth will be loosed in heaven." (Matthew 16:19)

The process of forgiveness involves removing all the strongholds and underlying sources that make forgiveness difficult. Underlying sources are: unhealed hurts, unmet needs, and unresolved issues.

V) THE FORGIVENESS PROCESS: To and through the cross

Who do I need to forgive?

- Another person
- God
- Self

Process

- Binding and loosing
- Inner healing
- Steps to forgiveness
- Repentance: one key to forgiveness: (Ezekiel 18:30–32)

VI) <u>**WALKING IN COMPLETE FORGIVENESS**</u>

1 Corinthians 13:4–8a:

"Love is patient, love is kind. It does not envy, it does not boast, it is not proud. It is not rude, it is not self-seeking, it is not easily angered, it keeps no record of wrongs. Love does not delight in evil but rejoices with the truth. It always protects, always trusts, always hopes, and always perseveres. Love never fails."

FORGIVENESS AT THE CROSS

Dear Father,

Please uncover areas of unforgiveness in my heart and help me to release them to you. I choose to forgive those who have been used to wound me, because I want more of you.

(Say out loud the names of those who have offended you. See them as victims of Satan's manipulation to hurt you, and release them by saying that you forgive them and release them to Jesus. Pray for them and bless them. Now, be free.)

Amen.

SMALL GROUP DISCUSSION
PRAYERS
Forgiveness

1) Who do I need to forgive?

_____

_____

_____

2) What blocks me from being willing to forgive someone? Even myself?

_____

_____

_____

PRAYERS FOR FORGIVENESS & REPENTANCE

Forgiving Another
"Lord, I forgive (or desire to forgive) _____. I give you permission to take the judgment and bitterness out of my life. I do not want this in my life anymore. I surrender it to you and ask you to remove it. I ask you to heal me where I have been wounded, to forgive me where I have sinned. I choose not to blame or hold the actions of others against them. I hereby surrender my right to be paid back for my loss, by the one who has sinned against me, and, in doing so, I declare my trust in God, alone, as the Righteous Judge. Father God, bless them in every way. In Jesus' Name. Amen. (Can be adapted to forgive self for sins against self.)

Forgiveness at the Cross
"Father God, I bring myself and _____ to the foot of the cross, and I ask you to help me to forgive him/her. I lay down all my anger, my hurt, my judgment, my need to blame, my desire to be paid back, my right to be right, and my desire to hear an apology. I surrender myself to you, and I ask you to help me to love _____ the way you love him/her, without any conditions on your love. Fill me to overflowing with your grace and your mercy, which will allow me to be a vessel of your love and forgiveness to him/her. Forgive me, Lord, for the grudges I have held and for withholding your love for him/her. I choose to forgive myself as well and will walk in a new way with your help. All of this I ask in Jesus' Name. Amen. (Can be adapted to forgive self at the cross.)

Forgiveness of God
Dear Father God, I have been angry with you. I have blamed you for the hard things in my life that I felt that you could have prevented. I have felt abandoned by you. I have failed to see your hand at work in my life for my good. I have lost my trust in you as I have struggled to understand the "whys" of my life. Forgive me, Lord, for turning my back on you, for hardening my heart to you. I need you, Lord, and I want to love you as you love me. Help me to know your love even deeper in my life. Thank you for never leaving me nor forsaking me. Thank you for your love and your mercy. I receive them now. In Jesus' Name. Amen.

Binding and Loosing Prayer
I bind myself to the mind of Christ and to His obedience to the will and purposes of God. I bind myself to the heart of Jesus that loved each of God's children enough to die for them. I bind myself to the finished work of the cross and to the unconditional forgiveness that flows through the blood of Jesus. I loose from myself my anger, my unforgiveness, my judgments, my wrong attitudes, my wrong patterns of thinking, and my wrong agreements about the other person. I loose my need to be right and my need to blame. I bind my feet to the path of God's righteousness that I might walk through the process of true forgiveness until I am set free in Jesus' Name. Amen.

Prayer of Repentance
Father God, I repent for _____. It is my desire to walk in your will and plan for my life. I commit my will to return to you. I ask your help to change my ways.
Jesus, I need you as my Savior. I humbly ask that you bathe me in Your Christ light that I may see your leading. Renew my mind in yours, Jesus that I may bring my entire thoughts captive to you. Empower my heart to love and to forgive myself and others as you have forgiven.
Holy Spirit, guide me each day to awareness of my desire to change. I need your empowerment to fill me with hope that change is possible. I come before the Cross of Salvation and ask for the protection of the blood of Jesus. Amen.

Prayer of Renouncing

Lord, I renounce _____ in the name of Jesus and by His shed blood. With the help of the Holy Spirit, I promise you that I will not engage in this sin anymore. By Your authority in me, I loose myself of this sin and cast it out of my life, never to return. I loose any destructive spirit that is connected to this sin and any wrong thoughts, beliefs, or behaviors that I have engaged in, casting them out of my life forever. I ask your forgiveness, Jesus, and thank you for your everlasting love for me. I want to love you more and more. Amen.

SCRIPTURAL REFERENCES
REPENTANCE & FORGIVENESS

"God made Him who had no sin to be sin for us, so that in Him we might become the righteousness of God." (2 Corinthians 5:21)

"This righteousness from God comes through faith in Jesus Christ to all who believe. There is no difference, for all have sinned and fall short of the glory of God, and are justified freely by His grace through the redemption that came by Christ Jesus. God presented Him as a sacrifice of atonement, through faith in His blood." (Romans 3:22–25a)

"I am not ashamed of the gospel, because it is the power of God for the salvation of everyone who believes." (Romans 1:16)

"For if you forgive men when they sin against you, your heavenly Father will also forgive you. But if you do not forgive men their sins, your Father will not forgive your sins." (Matthew 6:14–15)

"And when you stand praying, if you hold anything against anyone, forgive him, so that your Father in heaven may forgive you your sins." (Mark 11:25–26)

"Forgive us our debts, as we also have forgiven our debtors." (Matthew 6:12)

"In anger his master turned him over to the jailers to be tortured, until he should pay back all he owed. This is how my heavenly Father will treat each of you unless you forgive your brother from your heart." (Matthew 18:34–35)

"Do not be deceived, God is not mocked; for whatever a man sows, this he will also reap." (Galatians 6:7)

"Who may ascend into the hill of the Lord? And who may stand on His holy place? He who has clean hands and a pure heart." (Psalm 24:3–4)

"This day I call heaven and earth as witnesses against you that I have set before you life and death, blessings and curses. Now choose life, so that you and your children may live and that you may love the Lord your God. Listen to His voice, and hold fast to Him. For the Lord is your life, and He will give you many years in the land He swore to give to your fathers, Abraham, Isaac, and Jacob." (Deuteronomy 30:19–20)

"Do not repay evil with evil or insult with insult, but with blessing, because to this you were called so that you may inherit a blessing." (1 Peter 3:9)

"For God so loved the world that He gave His one and only Son, that whoever believes in Him shall not perish but have eternal life." (John 3:16)

"I will give you the keys of the kingdom of heaven; whatever you bind on earth will be bound in heaven and whatever you loose on earth will be loosed in heaven." (Matthew 16:19)

"Those who look to Him are radiant; their faces are never covered with shame." (Psalm 34:5)

"In repentance and rest is your salvation, in quietness and trust is your strength." (Isaiah 30:15)

"Produce fruit in keeping with repentance." (Luke 3:8a)

"God's kindness leads you toward repentance." (Romans 2:4)

"You do not delight in sacrifice, or I would bring it; you do not take pleasure in burnt offerings. The sacrifices of God are a broken spirit; a broken and contrite heart, O God, You will not despise." (Psalm 51:16–17)

"Love is patient, love is kind. It does not envy, it does not boast, it is not proud. It is not rude, it is not self-seeking, it is not easily angered, it keeps no record of wrongs. Love does not delight in evil but rejoices with the truth. It always protects, always trusts, always hopes, always perseveres. Love never fails."
(1 Corinthians 13:4–8a)

Notes:

Chapter 6 Outline

Authority And Spiritual Warfare

> **Key Concepts:**
> - **Spiritual Warfare**
> - **Does Satan Have Legal Ground?**
> - **All Authority in Jesus Christ**
> - **Christ's Authority within the Believer**
> - **Weapons of Warfare**

I) <u>SPIRITUAL WARFARE</u>

"For our struggle is not against flesh and blood, but against the rulers, against the authorities, against the powers of this dark world and against spiritual forces of evil in the heavenly realms." (Ephesians 6:12)

What is spiritual warfare?
- The act of joining God in the battle against Satan and his evil forces (demons) in the heavenly realms.
- Satan in Hebrew means "accuser," and he is constantly accusing and harassing God's people.
- Satan's purpose is our destruction!

"Your enemy the devil prowls around like a roaring lion looking for someone to devour." (1 Peter 5:8b)

"The thief comes only to steal and kill and destroy." (John 10:10)

"He (Satan) was a murderer from the beginning, not holding to the truth, for there is no truth in him. When he lies, he speaks his native language, for he is a liar and the father of lies." (John 8:44b)

First offensive move: Take Jesus as our Lord and Savior.

NEWS FLASH:

**THE BATTLE HAS ALREADY BEEN WON
BY JESUS CHRIST!**

"And having disarmed the powers and authorities, he made a public spectacle of them, triumphing over them by the Cross." (Colossians 2:15)

So if the battle has already been won, why are we fighting?

II) DOES SATAN HAVE LEGAL GROUND IN MY LIFE?

LEGAL GROUND: When are Christians vulnerable to spiritual attack by Satan?

Legal ground refers to those areas in our lives where we are linked to evil or deception either knowingly or without our knowledge. They are places within our soul that have not been healed. Legal ground includes the following:

- Bitterness and bitter-root judgments
- Cult or occult involvement of self or ancestors
- Generational ties and/or inherited curses
- Inner vows or slogans
- Spiritual adultery
- Wrong soul ties
- Deception: lie we believe; our willful choice
- Sins of the flesh
- Unforgiveness

Bitterness and bitter-root judgments:

Bitter roots are our sinful responses and our accusing judgments of people, and our rejection, unwillingness, and inability to forgive.

Bitter root judgments usually have to do with our parents or with early important relationships in our lives. Even though the judgements are showing up now in a person's relationship, especially spouses with each other, you will discover that the root to these present judgments are found early in their lives. Track the fruit to the root.

What is a Cult?

Cults teach some other way than Jesus to salvation, (John 14:6) and believe that salvation comes through keeping the teachings of the cult, not through the Messiah, Jesus Christ of Nazareth. Cults also may teach that Jesus did not come in the flesh. (1 John 4:1–2)

Characteristics of cults:

- Use psychological coercion to recruit, indoctrinate, and retain members.
- Form elitist society.
- Founder is self-appointed, dogmatic, messianic, not accountable, and has charisma.
- Believes the end justifies the means.
- Its wealth does not benefit its members or society.

Examples of Cults: Scientology, Unification Church, etc.

What is the Occult?

Occult—*"that which is hidden, secret or concealed; matters involving the supernatural"* (*Webster's New Collegiate Dictionary*). Occult refers to the *practice* of dealings with the world of spirits or spiritual forces other than the Triune Godhead.

Characteristics: psychological coercion; founder self-appointed, etc.

Examples of occult practices: Witchcraft, Wicca, etc

III) <u>ALL AUTHORITY IN JESUS CHRIST</u>

God has given a glorious inheritance for all believers through Jesus Christ. Our inheritance (we are co-heirs with Christ) includes dominion over all the works of darkness (sickness, disease, spiritual death, etc.). This glorious inheritance is for all believers.

"Then Jesus came to them and said, 'All authority in heaven and on earth has been given to Me.'" (Matthew 28:18)

"And He is the head of the body, the church; He is the beginning and the first born from among the dead, so that in everything He might have the supremacy. For God was pleased to have all His fullness dwell in Him." (Colossians 1:18–19)

"How God anointed Jesus of Nazareth with the Holy Spirit and power, and how He went around doing good and healing all who were under the power of the devil. Because God was with Him." (Acts 10:38)

"With authority and power He gives orders to evil spirits and they come out." (Luke 4:36b,)

IV) <u>CHRIST'S AUTHORITY WITHIN THE BELIEVER</u>

"I have given you authority to trample on snakes and scorpions and to overcome all the powers of the enemy; nothing will harm you." (Luke 10:19)

Jesus Christ through the power of the Holy Spirit has given us authority to cast out demons to overcome the powers of the enemy. Authority commands! Authority is not about begging or asking. And here we are told to do this work ourselves through Christ. We are told to CAST them out!

Matthew 8:8–9, 13: "The centurion answered and said, 'Lord, I am not worthy that you should come under my roof: but speak the word only, and my servant shall be healed. For I am a man under authority, having soldiers under me: and I say to this man, "Go," and he goes; and to another, "Come," and he comes; and to my servant, "Do this," and he does it. . . And Jesus said to the centurion, 'Go your way; and as you have believed, so be it done unto you.' And his servant was healed in the same hour."

God's authority is exercised through Gods Word spoken through us. We are His hands, His voice, and His feet on this earth. God's Word states that the power of life and death are in the spoken word: Proverbs 18:21, "Death and life are in the power of the tongue: and they that love it shall eat the fruit thereof."

Other Scriptures: Colossians 2:9–10; Isaiah 54:17; 2 Corinthians 10:4–6; Romans 8:31; 1 John 5:4.

V) <u>WEAPONS OF WARFARE: ARMOR OF GOD</u>

"Finally, be strong in the Lord and in his mighty power. Put on the **full armor of God** so that you can take your stand against the devils schemes. For our struggle is not against flesh and blood, but against the rulers, against the authorities, against the powers of this dark world and against the spiritual forces of evil in the heavenly realms. Therefore put on the full armor of God, so that when the day of evil comes, you may be able to stand your ground, and after you have done everything, to stand. **Stand firm** then, with the **belt of truth** buckled around your waist, with the **breastplate of righteousness** in place, and with your **feet fitted with the readiness that comes from the gospel of peac**e. In addition to all this, take up **the shield of faith**, with which you can extinguish all flaming arrows of the evil one. Take the **helmet of salvation** and the **sword of the Spirit**, which is the word of God. And **pray in the Spirit** on all occasions with all kinds of prayer and requests." (Ephesians 6:10–18)

WE ARE COVERED FROM HEAD TO TOE
WITH JESUS!!!

How do we enter the battle with full confidence of victory?
- Repent of our sins, renounce, and turn from them
- Receive healing in our souls from unhealed hurts, unmet needs, and unresolved issues
- Receive forgiveness and cleansing through the Blood of Jesus Christ and forgive others
- Walk in truth and love in the authority of Jesus Christ

PROCLAIMING THE WORD OF GOD

Victory Scriptures:

Romans 8:37—More than a conqueror through Christ Jesus.

Ephesians 2:8—Saved by grace through faith.

2 Corinthians 10:5—Bringing every thought captive to God.

3 John 1:2—Prospering in health in your soul.

Isaiah 10:27—The anointing breaks the yoke of bondage.

Matthew 5:14—Through Christ, an expression of Jesus' light to the world.

Luke 10:19—You have power over the enemy's power.

John 14:12—"Greater works will you do," says Jesus.

1 John 2:27—The anointing abides in you.

Jeremiah 20:11–12—Those who persecute you will not prosper.

Isaiah 54:17—No weapon formed against you will prosper.

1 John 4:4—Jesus who is in you is greater than the enemy in the world.

Colossians 2: 15—Satan was stripped of his power.

Revelation 12:11—You are an overcomer by the Blood of the Lamb
and by the word of your testimony.

PRAISE AND WORSHIP

"After consulting the people, Jehoshaphat appointed men to sing to the Lord and to praise Him for the splendor of His holiness as they went out at the head of the army, saying: 'Give thanks to the Lord, for His love endures forever.' **As they began to sing and praise,** the Lord set ambushes against the men of Ammon and Moab and Mount Seir who were invading Juda, and **they were defeated.**" (2 Chronicles 20:21–22)

"May the praise of God be in their mouths and a double-edged sword in their hands, to inflict vengeance on the nations and punishment on the peoples, to bind their kings with fetters, their nobles with shackles of iron, to carry out the sentence written against them. This is the glory of all His saints. Praise the Lord." (Psalm 149:6–9)

"Praise be to the Lord my Rock, who trains my hands for war, my fingers for battle. He is my loving God and my fortress, my stronghold and my deliverer, my shield in whom I take refuge, who subdues peoples under me." (Psalm 144:1–2)

"When a woman who had lived a sinful life...she brought an alabaster jar of perfume and as she stood before Him at His feet weeping, she began to wet His feet with her tears. Then she wiped them with her hair, kissed them and pour perfume on them....Jesus said to the her, 'Your sins are forgiven.'" (Luke 7:37–38, 48)

"Be very careful, then, how you live...be filled with the Spirit. Speak to one another with psalms, hymns, and spiritual songs. Sing and make music in your heart to the Lord, always giving thanks to God the Father for everything, in the name of our Lord Jesus Christ." (Ephesians 5:15a, 18b–20)

OBEDIENCE TO GOD

"Observe therefore all the commands I am giving you today, so that you may have the strength to go in and take over the land that you are crossing the Jordan to possess, and so that you may live long in the land that the Lord swore to your forefathers to give to them and their descendants, a land flowing with milk and honey." (Deuteronomy 11:8–9, NIV)

See: Deuteronomy 12:32; 2 Corinthians 10:4–6, NIV; 1 Peter 1:14–16 John 14:23, NIV; 1 John 2:5–6

BINDING AND LOOSING PRAYER

(Concept from Liberty Savard's Trilogy *Shattering Your Strongholds*, *Breaking the Power*, and *Producing the Promise*.)

"I will give you the keys to the kingdom of heaven; whatever you bind on earth will be bound in heaven, and whatever you loose on earth will be loosed in heaven." (Matthew 16:19)

To Bind: to knit, fasten, tie, weave together, wind around, cause to coalesce, to join together, and to become one again.

To Loose: break up, destroy, dissolve, unloose, melt, put off, wreck, crack to sunder by separation of the parts, shatter into minute fragments, disrupt, lacerate, convulse with spasms, break forth, burst, rend, and tear.

We are to bind ourselves, our mind, our thoughts, our heart, our will, and our emotions to Jesus Christ, and to the finished work of the Cross.

And we are to loose off all hurtful judgments, ungodly thoughts, personal agendas, wrongful attitudes, negative desires, and false beliefs, and the strongholds that protect them.

DELIVERANCE PRAYER

Deliverance prayer is another weapon God has given us for spiritual warfare. Deliverance refers to the form of prayer whereby "spirits or demons' are named and "cast off" of the person being prayed for by the authority of Christ within those who are praying. The individual being prayed for renounces these spirits of darkness in deliverance prayer, also through Christ's authority.

"And these signs will accompany those who believe: in my name they will drive out demons . . ." (Mark 16: 17a and see Luke 4:36b)

Christians will be harassed and even temporarily invaded by Satan and his demons, but this is not "possession" by an evil spirit. Only non-Christians (anyone who has not accepted Jesus Christ) can be possessed. Exorcism is praying for non-Christians to be set free from evil spirits.

Many times it is better to begin with inner healing prayer before praying for deliverance.

Some types of deliverance prayer:

- Renouncing the influence of cult involvement and the influence of occult involvement; compulsive, immoral sexual activity; addictive behaviors; specific evil spirits (i.e., fear, anxiety, disease, judgment, rage, perversion, pride, torment, depression, lying, etc.).
- Breaking wrong soul ties (sexual, possessive, soul, etc.), inner vows or word curses.

Following deliverance prayer:

- Assure the person of God's mercy, forgiveness, and love for him/her.
- Pray for the person to be filled by the Holy Spirit in all places where healing and deliverance have occurred.
- After the person leaves, pray a cleansing prayer over the area and over the prayer team.
- Thank God for His authority and sovereignty over all things in this world.

SMALL GROUP DISCUSSION
QUESTIONS and PRAYERS
Authority and Spiritual Warfare

1) What part(s) of this teaching on spiritual warfare was new for you? How do you feel about what you were taught?

   _____

   _____

   _____

2) Share a place of challenge that you have struggled to gain authority over in your spiritual walk.

   _____

   _____

   _____

3) What other spiritual experiences or religions have you tried in your search for God? Have you renounced any of these that were not Christian?

   _____

   _____

   _____

4) How have you used the Word of God to stand strong against the attack of the enemy?

   _____

   _____

   _____

APPENDIX

I. <u>Putting on the Armor of God–Ephesians 6:13–18</u>

Lord, I gratefully put on the armor you provided for me, that I might be ready to do your will.

I put on the **<u>Helmet of Salvation</u>**. It covers my mind, thoughts, and what I dwell on. Casting down every vain imagination that exalts itself against you, I bring every thought captive to the Lord Jesus Christ. For your word says "I have the mind of Christ."

It covers my eyes, what I see, look at and perceive. Your Word says, "If the eye be single the whole body be full of light," and my eyes are singly on you, Lord.

It covers my ears, what I hear, listen to, and understand. Your Word says, "My sheep hear my voice and no other will they follow."

It covers my nose. I can smell the sweet fragrance of your presence, Lord, The Rose of Sharon and The Lilly of the Valley. I can also smell the evil sulfurous odor of Satan.

It covers my mouth, what I speak, declare, and proclaim. Your Word says, "Life and death are in the tongue," and I choose life.

It also covers my neck, which is not stiff and arrogant toward you, but yielded and humble.

Thank you, Lord, for your Helmet of Salvation, the Precious Blood of Jesus. It covers every entrance place into me.

I put on the **<u>Breastplate of Righteousness</u>**. It covers my filthiness with your Righteousness and brings me into right standing with God the Father. It keeps my emotions in balance with Jesus, and covers my heart, which is deceitful above all things. I ask you to "Search me, Oh God, and know my heart, try me and know my thoughts, and see if there be any wickedness in me, and lead me in the Way everlasting." Create in me a clean heart, Oh God, and renew in me a right spirit. Cast me not from Thy presence and take not the Holy Spirit from me." I want to have clean hands and a pure heart that I might come before you.

I put on the **<u>Belt of Truth</u>** around my loins, my birthing place, my mind, where I think, my mouth, where I speak, my heart, where the issues of life are, and my emotions, where I feel, so that I am girded about in truth. For if you know the Truth, the Truth will set you free.

I put on the **<u>Shoes of the Gospel of Peace</u>** that I might be ready to do your will; to go to the left, to the right, straight ahead, or turn around: to stand still, walk, or run at your bidding. I will take back the territory the enemy has stolen, and bring the Gospel of Peace, Love, and Forgiveness to all you put in my path.

I take up the **<u>Shield of Faith</u>** to ward off the fiery darts of the enemy. Increase my faith in you and perfect and complete that faith to your honor and glory.

I take up the **<u>Sword of the Spirit</u>**, which is the Word of God. It is sharper than any two-edged sword, to reveal first the intents and purposes of my heart, and then wherever you send it; to pierce the darkness, cut off evil, or prune for more fruit. Guide my hand, Lord, with your hand.

Thank you for the ability to **<u>pray in the Spirit at all times</u>**, to praise and worship you, to intercede or be in fellowship with you.

Over all, I put on the mantle of Love and the mantle of Humility, that all might be done in your perfect justice. Amen.

A Checklist for Areas of Bondage
(This is your confidential information.)

Occult Involvement
_ Read your horoscope or been involved in astrology?
_ Had your palm read, tea leaves or fortune told, (even read about or tried to do it yourself, or used tarot cards?
_ Practiced or studied levitation, telepathy, ESP, clairvoyance, automatic writing, astral projection (soul travel), water witching (use of divining rod or dousing rod)?
_ Been hypnotized or tried to induce hypnosis?
_ Used a Ouija board, crystal ball, eight ball, pendulum, or other fortune-telling tools?
_ Consulted a medium, been to a séance or spiritualist meeting?
_ Been a channeler (medium who contacts the dead: necromancy, Spiritism, Spiritualism)?
_ Read occult literature or psychic phenomena?
_ Have any pagan religious or occult objects or charm you trust rather than God?
_ Entered into a blood pact with anyone?
_ Cast a hex, magic spell, or asked someone else to do it for you?
_ Involved in magic or the black arts?
_ Seen occultist movies or programs (i.e., *The Lazarus Effect, Poltergeist, The Visit, Rosemary's Baby, Exorcist, Silence of the Lambs,* etc.)?

Cult Involvement
_ Believed in reincarnation?
_ Practiced I-Ching
_ "Mind Sciences"... EST, Scientology, "Mind Control," "Christian Mind Sciences," etc.?
_ New Age, yoga, TM, Eckankar, eastern meditation and chants, eastern Religions: (i.e., Buddhism, Zen Buddhism, Hinduism, Hare Krishna, Confucianism, Taoism, Swedenborgianism, Rosicrucianism, Branch Davidians, the Manson Family, Heaven's Gate, Peoples Temple, Scientology, Unification Church, Bhagwan Shree Rajineesh, Twelve Tribes, etc.).
_ Rejected or denied the Trinity, Jesus Christ as Son of God, His virgin birth, His blood atonement for sins, His resurrection in the body, His second coming?
_ Thought or taught all religions lead to God–all will be saved?

Sexual Involvement
_ Watched/seen pornographic movies, pictures, on TV/video, theatres, or on the Internet?
_ Read/seen pornographic novels, magazines, or books?
_ Been involved in sexual fantasy with masturbation, or any other compulsive, immoral sexual acts?
_ Been involved in any unbiblical sexual behavior: fornication, adultery, homosexual and bisexual acts, transsexual acts, transvestite, sadomasochistic acts, pedophilia, incest, group sex, sodomy, bestiality, prostitution?

Addictions
_ Addicted to alcohol, barbiturates, amphetamines, cocaine, or other drugs and chemicals.
_ Ever taken LSD, mescaline, any other mind-expanding drugs, or smoked marijuana, glue,

Jesus came to set the captives free. Do not be entangled again with a yoke of bondage!
Galatians 5:1; Deuteronomy 18:10–13; 1 Corinthians 6:9–11; Matthew 18:6; James 1:12–16; Exodus 20:3; Romans 1:24–32; Deuteronomy 27:21

Notes:

Chapter 7 Outline

Where's The Power?

> **Key Concepts:**
> - **The Person of the Holy Spirit**
> - **Gifts of the Godhead**
> - **Generational Bondages & Strongholds**
> - **Receive Power to become My Witnesses**
> - **Releasing the Holy Spirit**

Acts 1:8—"But you <u>shall</u> <u>receive power</u> when the Holy Spirit has come upon you; and <u>you shall be witnesses to Me</u> in Jerusalem, and in all Judea and Samaria, and to the end of the earth." (NKJV)

I)   THE PERSON OF THE HOLY SPIRIT
The Holy Spirit has the characteristics of a Person:

- Mind, Will, Feeling
- Activities
- Relationship with Human Beings
- Divine Attributes of the Godhead
- Names

The Holy Spirit is the expressed power of the Trinity.
Christian liberty stems from the work of the Holy Spirit:
"Where the Spirit of the Lord is, there is liberty" (2 Corinthians 3:17).

II)   GIFTS OF THE GODHEAD
"Be filled with the Spirit" (Ephesians 5:18)
Each member of the Godhead plays a role in giving gifts to mankind. See appendix at the end of this chapter.

III)   RECEIVING POWER

POWER COMES UPON YOU

Acts 1:8—"But you shall **receive power** when the Holy Spirit has come upon you; and you shall be witnesses to Me in Jerusalem, and in all Judea and Samaria, and to the end of the earth." (NKJV)

POWER OVERSHADOWS YOU

Luke 1:35—"And the angel answered and said to her, '**The Holy Spirit will come upon you, and the power of the Highest will overshadow you**; therefore, also, that Holy One who is to be born will be called the Son of God. (NKJV)

POWER ENDUES YOU

Luke 24:49—"Behold, **I send the Promise of My Father upon you**; but **tarry** in the city of Jerusalem **until you are endued** with power from on high." (NKJV)

POWER UNITES US

Acts 2:1–4

1   "Now when the Day of Pentecost had fully come, they were all with one accord in one place.
2   And suddenly there came a sound from heaven, as of a rushing mighty wind, and it filled the whole house where they were sitting.
3   Then there appeared to them divided tongues, as of fire, and one sat upon each of them.
4   And they were all filled with the Holy Spirit and began to speak with other tongues, as the Spirit gave them utterance." (NKJV)

QUOTE: Jim Elliot

"He makes His ministers a flame of fire. Am I ignitable? God deliver me from the dread asbestos of 'other things.' Saturate me with the oil of the Spirit that I may be aflame. But flame is transient, often short lived. Canst thou bear this, my soul—short life? . . . Make me thy fuel, Flame of God."

IV)   RELEASE OF THE HOLY SPIRIT WITHIN YOU:
1)   First you must be born again. (Romans 8:9)
2)   You have to ask. (Luke 11:8)
3)   You have to surrender. (Romans 12:1)
4)   Repent and confess sins. (Repentance when used as a noun is *metanoia*, which means "a change of mind.") (Acts 3:19)
5)   You must be willing to obey the Holy Spirit. (Acts 5:32)
6)   You need to believe God. (Galatians 3:2)
7)   You have to exercise what God has given you. (Acts 2:4)

"But you shall receive power . . .to be (come) My witnesses. . ." (Acts 1:8, NKJV)

LARGE or SMALL GROUP
PRAYER FOR RELEASE OF THE HOLY SPIRIT
Where's the Power?

Come Holy Spirit, and baptize me with the fire of your love. I surrender to the best of my ability, and now I want to be filled with your Spirit. I need your power in my life. Please come, and fill me now. Lord, I believe that when I surrendered to you as my Lord, we became one. You are the vine and I am the branch of the vine. All that you are is within me. My life flows from you. I believe that as I yield and ask, you will release your strength, wisdom, healing, etc. to meet the needs of the hour. I yield now to receive your sanctification gifts of Isaiah 12:2: wisdom and understanding, counsel and might, knowledge and the fear of the Lord. I need these gifts in my life, to grow as a Christian. I yield and ask you to release your manifestation gifts of service, as listed in 1 Corinthians 12: wisdom, knowledge, faith, healing, miracles, prophecy, discernment, tongues, and interpretation of tongues. I need them to witness to a hurting world. Only in your power, guided by your Spirit, can my life be fruitful. Holy Spirit come. Holy Spirit come. I want it all, wrapped in the greatest gift of all: love.

"... the greatest of these is love" (1 Corinthians 13:13).

Melt me, mold me, fill me, use me. Give me opportunities to use your gifts to reveal your love and mercy. Stretch me, Lord. I will not limit your gifts by my perceptions of what I can handle. Holy Spirit, expand my capability. Work in me in a powerful way. I want every purpose God has for my life to be fulfilled, and I need you, mighty Spirit of God, to bring that purpose to fulfillment. Come Holy Spirit. Come.

As you flow through me to minister to others, I know that you are flowing within me to heal my life too. Thank you for flooding the deep places of my life with your electric love. Thank you for washing and cleansing any wounds and scars from the past that still have the power to dominate my thoughts and suppress my physical and emotional freedom. Thank you for bringing light into the shadows and warmth to any cold, dark rooms in my soul. Compassionate Holy Spirit, thank you for coming and drawing out the uncried tears, the unfinished grieving, the pain of loss, the traumas, the fear, the emotional hurts so painful that they were "buried alive." Spirit of Wisdom, thank you for coming into the root cause of any chronic failures. Gentle Holy Spirit, thank you for walking through my early years and facing the past with me. Thank you for reminding me that the love of Jesus was always there, filling in the gap between the love I needed and the love I received. (Thank the Holy Spirit for scanning your life and bringing to mind any hurtful memories that need to be healed. When they surface, simply say, "Holy Spirit I surrender that event to you for healing. Thank you for bringing your good out of the hurt (Romans 8:28). Praise you, Jesus.") Let this be an opportunity for a deeper release of the Holy Spirit as more of your emotional life becomes unbound.

Thank you, Holy Spirit, for your presence with me, flowing freely in me and through me. Thank you for being my friend, my teacher, my comforter, my counselor, my intercessor, and the giver of extravagant gifts. Thank you especially for _____ . (Continue thanking Him spontaneously.)

Close your eyes and sing, "Come, Holy Ghost," or "Spirit of the Living God," or another song that invites the Holy Spirit to come. Amen.

APPENDIX AND SCRIPTURES

GIFTS OF THE GODHEAD (source of information: Jack W Hayford, general editor, and Sam Middlebrook, (et al), *Spirit-filled Life Study Bible,* (computer file), electronic ed., Logos Library System, (Nasville: Thomas Nelson, 1991, 1997).

GIFTS OF THE FATHER
Romans 12:3–8: Gifts of the Father (Basic Life Purpose and Motivation)
  1. **PROPHECY**
      a. To speak with forthrightness and insight, especially when enabled by the Spirit of God (Joel 2:28).
      b. To demonstrate moral boldness and uncompromising commitment to worthy values.
      c. To influence others in one's arena of influence with a positive spirit of social or spiritual righteousness.
      NOTE: Because all three categories of gifts—the Father's, the Holy Spirit's—involve some expression of "prophecy," it is helpful to differentiate. In this category (Romans 12) the focus is *general,* characterized by that level of the prophetic gift that would belong to *every* believer—"all flesh." The Holy Spirit's "gift of prophecy" (1 Corinthians 12) refers to supernatural prompting, so much so that tongues with interpretation is equated with its operation (1 Corinithains 14:5). The office–gift of the prophet, which Christ gives to His church through individual ministries, is yet another expression of prophecy: those holding this gift must meet *both* the Old Testament requirements of a prophet's accuracy in his message, and the New Testament standards of life and character required of spiritual leadership.

  2. **MINISTRY**
      a. To minister and render loving, general service to meet the needs of others.
      b. Illustrated in the work and office of the deacon (Matthew 20:26).

  3. **TEACHING**
      a. The supernatural ability to explain and apply the truths received from God for the church.
      b. Presupposes study and the Spirit's illumination, which provides the ability to make divine truth clear to the people of God.
      c. Considered distinct from the work of the prophet who speaks as the direct mouthpiece of God.

  4. **EXHORTATION**
      a. Literally means "to call aside for the purpose of making an appeal."
      b. In a broader sense it means to entreat, comfort, or instruct (Acts 4:36; Hebrews 10:25).

  5. **GIVING**
      a. The essential meaning is to give out of a spirit of generosity.
      b. In a more technical sense, it refers to those with resources aiding those without such resources (2 Corinthians 8:2; 9:11–13).
      c. This gift is to be exercised without outward show or pride and with liberality. (2 Corinthians 1:12; 8:2; 9:11, 13)

  6. **LEADERSHIP**
      a. Refers to the one "standing in front."
      b. Involves the exercise of the Holy Spirit in modeling, superintending, and developing the body of Christ.
      c. Leadership is to be exercised with diligence.

7. **MERCY**
   a. To feel sympathy with the misery of another.
   b. To relate to others in empathy, respect, and honesty.
   c. To be effective, this gift is to be exercised with kindness and cheerfulness—not as a matter of duty.

GIFTS OF THE HOLY SPIRIT
1 Corinthians 12:8–10, 28: Gifts of the Holy Spirit
1. **WORD OF WISDOM**
   a. Supernatural perspective to ascertain the divine means for accomplishing God's will in given situations.
   b. Divinely given power to appropriate spiritual intuition in problem-solving.
   c. Sense of divine direction.
   d. Being led by the Holy Spirit to act appropriately in a given set of circumstances.
   e. Knowledge rightly applied: wisdom works interactively with knowledge and discernment.

2. **WORD OF KNOWLEDGE**
   a. Supernatural revelation of the divine will and plan.
   b. Supernatural insight or understanding of circumstances or a body of facts by revelation: that is, without assistance of any human resource but solely by divine aid.
   c. Implies a deeper and more advanced understanding of the communicated acts of God.
   d. Involves moral wisdom for right living and relationships.
   e. Requires objective understanding concerning divine things in human duties.
   f. May also refer to knowledge of God or of the things that belong to God, as related in the gospel.

3. **FAITH**
   a. Supernatural ability to believe God without doubt.
   b. Supernatural ability to combat unbelief.
   c. Supernatural ability to meet adverse circumstances with trust in God's messages and words.
   d. Inner conviction impelled by an urgent and higher calling.

4. **GIFTS OF HEALINGS**
   a. Refers to supernatural healing without human aid.
   b. May include divinely assisted application of human instrumentation and medical means of treatment.
   c. Does not discount the use of God's creative gifts.

5. **WORKING OF MIRACLES**
   a. Supernatural power to intervene and counteract earthly and evil forces.
   b. Literally means a display of power giving the ability to go beyond the natural.
   c. Operates closely with the gifts of faith and healings to bring authority over sin, Satan, sickness, and the binding forces of this age.

6. **PROPHECY**
   a. Divinely inspired and anointed utterance.
   b. Supernatural proclamation in a known language.
   c. Manifestation of the Spirit of God—not of intellect (1 Corinthians 12:7).
   d. May be possessed and operated by all who have the infilling of the Holy Spirit (1 Corinthians 14:31).

    e.   Intellect, faith, and will are operative in this gift, but its exercise is not intellectually based. It is calling forth words from the Spirit of God.

7. DISCERNING OF SPIRITS
    a.   Supernatural power to detect the realm of the spirits and their activities
    b.   Implies the power of spiritual insight—supernatural revelation of plans and purposes of the enemy and his forces.

8. DIFFERENT KINDS OF TONGUES (see appendix)
    a.   Supernatural utterance in languages not known to the speaker: these languages may be existent in the world, revived from some past culture, or "unknown" in the sense that they are a means of communication inspired by the Holy Spirit (Isaiah 28:11; Mark 16:17; Acts 2:4; 10:44–48; 19:1–7; 1 Corinthians 12:10, 28–31; 13:1–3; 14:2, 4–22, 26–32).
    b.   Serve as an evidence and sign of the indwelling and working of the Holy Spirit.

9. INTERPRETATION OF TONGUES
    a.   Supernatural power to reveal the meaning of tongues.
    b.   Functions not as an operation of the mind of man but as the mind of the Spirit.
    c.   Does not serve as a translation (interpreter never understands the tongue he is interpreting), but rather is a declaration of meaning.
    d.   Is exercised as a miraculous and supernatural phenomenon as are the gifts of speaking in tongues and the gift of prophecy.

GIFTS OF THE SON
Ephesians 4:11 (Also 1 Corinthians 12:28): Gifts of the Son (Facilitate and Equip the Body of the Church)
1. APOSTLES
    a.   In apostolic days, it referred to a select group chosen to carry out directly the ministry of Christ; included the assigned task given to a few to complete the sacred canon of the Holy Scriptures.
    b.   Implies the exercise of a distinct representative role of broader leadership given by Christ.
    c.   Functions as a messenger or spokesman of God.
    d.   In contemporary times, it refers to those who have the spirit of apostleship in remarkably extending the work of the church, opening fields to the gospel, and overseeing larger sections of the body of Jesus Christ.

2. PROPHET
    a.   A spiritually mature spokesman/proclaimer with a special, divinely focused message to the church or the world.
    b.   A person uniquely gifted at times with insight into future events.

3. EVANGELIST
    a.   Refers primarily to a special gift of preaching or witnessing in a way that brings unbelievers into the experience of salvation.
    b.   Functionally, the gift of evangelist operates for the establishment of new works, while pastors and teachers follow up to organize and sustain.
    c.   Essentially, the gift of evangelist operates to establish converts and to gather them spiritually and literally into the body of Christ.

4. **PASTOR/TEACHER**
   a. The word "pastor" comes from a root meaning "to protect," from which we get the word "shepherd."
   b. Implies the function of a shepherd/leader to nurture, teach, and care for the spiritual needs of the body.

5. MISSIONARY (some see "apostle" or "evangelist" in this light).
   a. Implies the unfolding of a plan for making the gospel known to all the world (Romans 1:16).
   b. Illustrates an attitude of humility necessary for receiving a call to remote areas and unknown situations (Isaiah 6:1–13).
   c. Connotes an inner compulsion to lead the whole world to an understanding of Jesus Christ (2 Corinthians 5:14–20).

Special Graces
1. **HOSPITALITY**
   a. Literally means to love, to do, or to do with pleasure.
   b. Illustrates Peter's notion of one of the two categories of gifts: 1) teaching, 2) practical service (1 Peter 4:10, 11).
   c. Was utilized in caring for believers and workers who visited to worship, work, and become involved in the body of Christ.
   d. Illustrated in the teaching of Jesus concerning judgment (Matthew 25:35, 40).

2. **CELIBACY (Matthew 19:10; 1 Corinthians 7:7–9, 27; 1 Timothy 4:3; Rev. 14:4).**
   a. The Bible considers marriage to be honorable and ordained of God
   b. Implies a special gift of celibacy, which frees the individual from the duties, pressures, and preoccupations of family life, allowing undivided attention to the Lord's work.

3. **MARTYRDOM (1 Peter 4:12, 13)**
   a. Illustrated in the spirit of Stephen (Acts 7:59, 60).
   b. Fulfilled in the attitude of Paul (2 Timothy 4:6–8).

EXPLANATION OF GIFT OF TONGUES: ("Holy Spirit and Gifts" by Paul Wilbur; *Spirit-Filled Life Bible*, Nashville: Thomas Nelson, 1991)

The twofold functions of "tongues" is for personal edification and for public exhortation.

"Tongues" functions as a sign of the Holy Spirit's presence. Jesus prophesied it as a sign (Mark 16:17), Paul referred to it as a sign (1 Corinthians 14:22), and Peter noted its uniformity as a sign–gift in confirming the validity of the Gentiles' experience in the Holy Spirit. (Compare Acts 10:44–46 with 11:16, 17 and 15:7–9). Thus, speaking with tongues is a properly expected sign, affirming the Holy Spirit's abiding presence and assuring the believer of an invigorated living witness. It is one *indication of* that fullness of the Spirit.

Tongues for Personal Edification
First, "speaking in tongues" is a private affair for self-edification (1 Corinthians 14:2–4). Thus, glossolalia is practiced devotionally by the believer in his most intimate and intercessory moments of communication with God as he is moved upon by the Holy Spirit. This "devotional" application may also be practiced by corporate agreement, in group gatherings where no Unbelievers or uninformed people are present (1 Cor. 14:23). In line with this understanding, the following reasons are propounded for speaking with tongues:
1. Speaking with tongues as the Holy Spirit gives utterance is the unique spiritual gift identified with the church of Jesus Christ. All other gifts, miracles, and spiritual manifestations were in evidence during

Old Testament times, before the Day of Pentecost. This new phenomenon came into evidence and became uniquely identified with the church and was ordained by God for the church (1 Corinthians 12:28; 14:21).

2. Speaking with tongues is a specific fulfillment of prophecies by Isaiah and Jesus. Compare Isaiah 28:11 with 1 Corinthians 14:21, and Mark 16:17 with Acts 2:4; 10:46; 19:6; and 1 Corinthians 14:5, 14–18, 39.

3. Speaking with tongues is a proof of the resurrection and glorification of Jesus Christ (John 16:7; Acts 2:26).

4. Speaking with tongues is an evidence of the baptism in or infilling of the Holy Spirit (Acts 2:4; 10:45, 46; 19:6).

5. Speaking with tongues is a spiritual gift for self-edification (1 Corinthians14:4; Jude 20).

6. Speaking with tongues is a spiritual gift for spiritual edification of the church when accompanied by interpretation (1 Corinthians14:5).

7. Speaking with tongues is a spiritual gift for communication with God in private worship (1 Corinthians 14:15).

8. Speaking with tongues is a means by which the Holy Spirit intercedes through us in prayer (Romans 8:26; 1 Corinthians 14:14; Ephesians 6:18).

9. Speaking with tongues is a spiritual means for rejoicing (1 Corinthians 14:15; Ephesians 5:18, 19).

10. Paul's application of Isaiah's prophecy seems to indicate that speaking with tongues is also intended as a means of "rest" or "refreshing" (Isaiah 28:12; 1 Cor. 14:21).

11. Tongues follow as one confirmation of the Word of God when it is preached (Mark 16:17, 20; 1 Corinthians 14:22).

Tongues for Public Exhortation

Turning to the second function of "tongues"—public exhortation—1 Corinthians 14 bases the gifts of the Spirit on the one sure foundation of love (1 Corinthians 14:1). Public "tongues" also call for integrity in practice as the key for the preservation of order in our fellowship and the worship services. Conceding that there have been those who have abused the gift as an occasion for fleshly pride, we must recognize that it can be a vital and valuable part of worship when placed in its proper setting for the edification of the body (1 Corinthians 14:12, 13).

However, the sincere Spirit-filled believer will not be preoccupied with this gift alone, for he sees it as only one of many gifts given for the "wholeness" of the church; therefore, he does not worship or meet with others just to speak in tongues for the mere sake of the practice itself. Such motivation would be immature, vain, and idolatrous. Rather, sincere believers gather to worship God and to be thoroughly equipped for every good work through the teaching of His Word (2 Timothy 3:16, 17). Consequently, the scripturally sensitive believer recognizes the following New Testament direction regarding spiritual gifts:

1. Speaking in "tongues" only edifies public worship when it is interpreted; thus, the worshiper is to pray for the interpretation, and if it is withheld, he keeps silent, unless someone who functions in the gift of interpretation is known to be present (1 Corinthians 14:5, 28).

2. The Spirit works only to edify; thus, whenever He is truly present all things are in order and devoid of embarrassment or uneasiness (1 Corinthians 14:26, 40).

3. The "spirits of the prophets are subject to the prophets" (1 Cor. 14:32). That is, each truly Spirit-filled person can exercise self-control; thus, confusion can and should be avoided so that decency with unity may prevail (1 Corinthians 14:40).

4. The basis of all gifts is love. Love, not the experience of a gift, is the qualifying factor for those who would exercise spiritual gifts. Thus, in the administration of spiritual authority in the local

congregation, the Word demands that we "judge" (1 Corinthians 14:29) to confirm that those who exercise gifts actually do "pursue love and desire spiritual gifts" (1 Corinthians 13:1–13; 14:1).

5. The Author and Dispenser of the gifts is the Holy Spirit, who divides them as He wills; thus, no gift becomes the exclusive possession of any believer for his personal edification and pride. Rather, the gifts are placed in the church to be exercised by the body for the mutual edification of the believers (1 Corintians 12:1–11) and as a means for expanded ministry.

6. The exercise of tongues is to be limited to sequences of two or three at the most (1 Cor. 14:27). While many hold this to be a rigid number, others understand it to be a guideline to keep the worship service in balance. In actuality, the Holy Spirit rarely moves beyond these limitations; however, on occasions, for special reasons to meet special needs, there may be more than one sequence of two or three appropriately spaced apart in a given service. The overarching guideline is, "Let all things be done decently and in order" (1 Corinthians 14:40).

Notes:

Chapter 8

Healing Prayers

Attitudes Prayer

Attitudes: (Miriam Webster Dictionary definition): "A settled way of thinking or feeling about someone or something, typically one that is reflected in a person's behavior."

- the way you think and feel about someone or something
- a feeling or way of thinking that affects a person's behavior
- a way of thinking and behaving that people regard as unfriendly, rude, etc.

Synonyms:
- view, viewpoint, outlook, perspective, stance, standpoint, position, inclination, temper, orientation, approach, reaction

Positive attitudes in alignment with Christ: Galatians 5:22–26 – love, joy, peace, patience, kindness, goodness, faithfulness, gentleness, self-control.

Negative attitudes not in alignment with Christ: hate, ungodly sorrow, war-like, impatient, coldness or indifference, evil, disloyal or false, harshness, rashness.

Prayer:

Lord Jesus I confess my wrong behaviors and habits_____

I confess my wrong attitude of _____.

Show me the root of this wrong attitude. Show me the trauma/event that led me to develop a wrong pattern of thinking, wrong ideas, wrong desires, wrong beliefs, and wrong behaviors. (Pause: Time of healing of memories).

Show me the unmet needs, the unhealed hurts, and unresolved issues in my life. Take me to the roots. Show me the truth. Heal me Lord at this deepest level. (You may need to deal with inner vows and/or word curses here.)

(After healing in these areas and forgiveness, loose these wrong behaviors and habits and their strongholds in the Name of Jesus Christ.)

I bind myself to desiring the attitudes and behaviors of Christ. I bind all my reactions and responses to the will of you, God. I bind myself to the will of you, God for my life including your path and your timing for me.

Thank you God for loosing off me destructive thinking, behaviors, and strongholds and binding me to you, your will, your way.

Amen.

Receiving Healing – Revised (2011)
Liberty Savard, *Breaking the Power*, p. 118)

Prayer for Yourself:

"Lord, I bind my body, soul and spirit to your will and purposes for my life. I know that my born-again spirit is connected to your mighty Spirit. I know that my unsurrendered soul is still resisting your will and purposes for my life in certain areas. I am using the Keys of the Kingdom to bring it into alignment with the purposes for which you created it. Thank you for the Keys of the Kingdom to use against my rebellious unsurrendered soul and against the works of the enemy.

"I have unhealthy needs in my physical body, the temple you have fashioned for me to dwell in—the same temple you have chosen to dwell in by your Holy Spirit. Lord, I know I cannot follow my wrong desires and choices and then expect you to heal the consequences of each ongoing disobedience. I loose deception and denial from my unsurrendered soul as I seek your truth. I want to be in good health to pursue you and the Kingdom work you have ordained for me to do.

"I bind my mind, will and emotions to your truth. I loose all resistance my unsurrendered soul has to any area of your Word. Holy Spirit, I ask you to be the watchman on the wall if I stumble or turn aside from walking in the will of the Father. Sound a warning in whatever way is necessary to quickly reveal my error.

"I loose any layers I have allowed my unsurrendered soul to lay down to protect its belief system. Let your mercy and grace fill me, Father. I don't seek just a deliverance from the symptoms of my physical infirmity, Lord—I want to know the source of this weakness within me. Show me if my symptoms are a result of soulish indulgence, an acceptance of and agreement with error, a spiritual attack, or an invasion into my body by an infectious organism.

"If these symptoms have been caused by a spiritual attack, Father, I loose the enemy's hindrances and devices from my life. If these symptoms have been caused by disobedience in my unsurrendered soul, I loose all stronghold thinking, denial, and deception from myself. I loose word curses, generational bondage thinking, and wrong teachings from myself.

"If this sickness has been caused by an infectious organism, show me the weakness in my immune system that has allowed it to find entrance into my body. Show me if I am eating wrong. Show me if I am relying on medications and man-made answers that are not in your will for me. Show me the source of the entrance that this thing found in me.

"I bind every cell of my body to your will and your plans and purposes. I loose the life out of any bacteria, virus, infection or mutated cell in my body and command it to die. I loose, smash, and destroy their reproductive ability. I loose all wrong beliefs, unforgiveness, and anger from my unsurrendered soul that have been contributing to any weakness in my body's immune system. I ask you to reveal any other sources of physical vulnerability in me. Thank you for your care and for the Keys. In Jesus' Name, Amen."

Prayer for Others
(**First pray this for yourself**)
(Adapted from Liberty Savard, *Breaking the Power*, p. 108)

Prayer for Others:

In the Name of Jesus Christ, I bind _____'s will to the will of God. I bind _____'s mind to the mind of Christ and his/her emotions to the healing balance and comfort of the Holy Spirit.

In the Name of Jesus Christ, I loose the effects and influences of wrong agreements that _____ has been a part of. I loose wrong beliefs and mind sets off _____'s unsurrendered soul is hanging onto. I loose the deception and confusion of _____'s coping mechanisms and wrong behaviors, and I loose (destroy) the works of the enemy from him or her. (1 John 3:8).

Thank you that you have given me the Keys and the authority to do so. Thank you, Lord, for the truth. Amen.

Matthew 16:19, NIV: *"I will give you the keys to the kingdom of heaven; whatever you bind on earth will be bound in heaven, and whatever you loose on earth will be loosed in heaven."*

BREAKING GENERATIONAL TIES

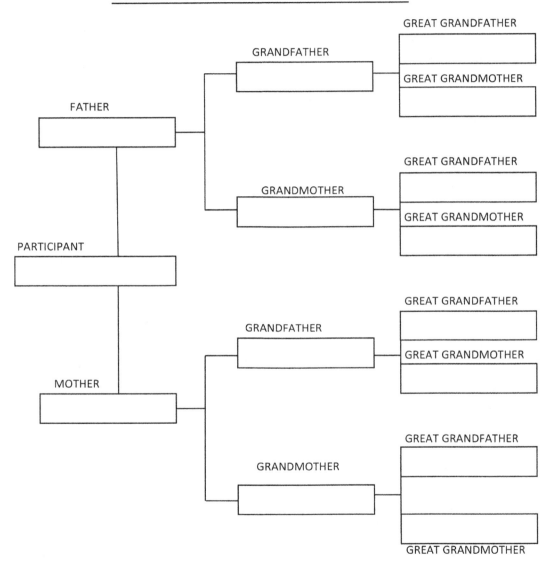

Forgiveness Prayer at the Cross

Dear Lord,

Your Word says that as I forgive others, I too am forgiven.

Here at the cross I choose to forgive.

(Name the one you are forgiving)_____

I forgive you for hurting me. What you did was wrong. You hurt me. But I release you from my judgment. I set you free to Jesus Christ and I am set free too. Thank You, Jesus.

(Allow time for this. Let Jesus show you how He is with that person who hurt you. There may be a need for you to ask for forgiveness of the other.)

(Do this with as many as the Holy Spirit brings before you.)

Amen.

Prayer of Renouncement and Forgiveness

Father,

I confess to you my involvement and participation in (name sin).

I renounce specifically (name behaviors):

I understand that such things are an abomination to you and are detestable in your sight.

I humbly ask your forgiveness for my sin in these areas.

I ask You to remove any demonic entrance in me as the result of my actions or other's sinful actions on me and to cleanse me from these sins and close all doorways forever with the precious blood of Jesus.

I ask this in the name of Jesus and thank you for it.

In the name of Jesus Christ, I command these demonic spirits to go away and never return. I now, by faith, close every doorway of those areas of sin in my life.

Now, Father, please fill me in these areas with your Holy Spirit.

I thank you, in Jesus' name.

Amen. (Prayer credit to Rita Bennett, *Emotionally Free*)

How to Receive God's Love and Plan for Salvation

- **Acknowledge** the problem (separation from God because of sin).
- **Admit** to being a sinner, and that you need salvation.
- **Confess** your sins
- **Recognize** that Jesus Christ died on the cross for your sins.
- **Commit** yourself to Jesus Christ so that He can save and guide you.
- **Receive** Jesus Christ as your personal Savior and Lord, now.

  "That if you confess with your mouth Jesus is Lord, and believe in your Heart that God raised Him from the dead, you will be saved." Romans 10:9

  "For whoever will call on the name of the Lord will be saved."

Prayer to Receive Jesus Christ

Lord Jesus, I know that I have sinned against you and that I am not living according to your plan; therefore, I ask you to forgive me. I believe that you died for me, and in doing so, you paid the debt for my sins. I repent of my sin, and now I want to live the kind of life that you want me to live. I ask you to come into my life and be my personal Savior: Help me to follow you and to obey you as my Lord. Allow me to discover your good and perfect will for my life. Amen.

Jesus Saves New Testament, Copyright 1999 by The Lockman Foundation, La Habra, California.

I AM

I am made in God's image. Gen. 1:26

I am born of God. 1 John 5:18

I am led by the Spirit of the Living God. Rom 8:14

I am a temple of the Holy Spirit. 1 Cor. 6:19

I am not my own. 1 Cor. 6:19

I am bought with a price. 1 Cor. 7:23

I am full of the love of God. Rom 5:5

I am forgiven. Col. 1:14

I am walking in love. Eph. 5:2

I am at peace with God through my Lord Jesus Christ. Rom 5:1

I am fully persuaded what He's promised, He's able to do. Rom 4:21

I am not under the law, but under grace. Rom 6:16

I am free from the law of sin and death. Rom 8:2

I am walking in newness of the spirit. Rom 7:6

I am giving my Father joy because I'm walking in truth. 1 John 1:14

I am worth the body and blood of Jesus. Luke 22:18–19

I am receiving the unconditional love of God. Rom. 5:8

I am seated in heavenly places in Christ Jesus Eph. 2:6

I am a saint. Eph. 1:1

I am accepted. Eph. 1:6

I am greatly loved. Dan 10:19

I am precious in the sight of the Lord. Ps. 116:16

I am a servant. Ps. 116:1

I am listened to by God my Father. Ps 116:1

I am dead to sin. Rom. 6:11

I am alive unto God through Jesus Christ my Lord. Rom. 6:11

I am free from condemnation. Rom 8:1

I am giving thanks in all things. Phil. 4:6

I am laying aside all malice, envy, evil speaking. 1 Peter 2:1

I am partaking of God's divine nature. 1 Peter 2:1

I am not a victim, but an overcomer. Rev. 12:11

I am fashioned by the Master's hand. Eph. 2:10

I am a value to God. Matt. 10:31

I am walking in great peace, because I love God's law (of love), and nothing does offend me. Ps 119:165

I am predestined to be conformed to the image of His Son. Rom. 8:29

I am wise in heart. Prov. 10:8

I am an overcomer by the blood of the Lamb and word of my testimony. Rom 12:11

I am healed by His stripes. Is. 53:5

I am strong in the Lord and power of His might. Eph. 6:10

The Lord's Prayer
(Prayed as Intercession for Self or Another)

Abba, Daddy in heaven. I lift up and respect your Holy name. You are my Father. You are my protector and I am held in your arms.

I pray your kingdom come into the life of (me or name of person), and that your will be done in (my or name of person) life here on earth as it is in heaven.

Today, give (me, or name of person) your daily bread—physically and spiritually. Your living Word in (me or name of person).Fill me with all I need.

Forgive (me, or name of person) his/her sins as (I or name of person) forgive/s those who have sinned against him/her. (I confess my own sins now before you, Father.)

Heal (me or name of person) soul (add "and spirit" if the person is not a Christian) that (I or name of person) may be able to forgive others and forgive (myself or him/herself).

Good Shepherd, pastor of our souls, lead (me or name of person) away from all evil, dear Father.

Protect us all from the attacks of the enemy. You are my stronghold and a very present help.

For yours, dear Father, is the kingdom and the power and the glory forever.

According to your Word, let it be so in Jesus' name. Amen.

(Scripture reference: Matthew 6:9–13)

Breaking Wrong Sexual and Psychological Soul Ties

Do you realize that your bodies are part of Christ?

Should a man's body, which belongs to Christ, be joined it to a prostitute? Never! Don't you know that if a man joins himself to a prostitute or fornicator, he becomes one body with her? Should a woman's body which belongs to Christ, be joined to a fornicator? If you join with that man outside of marriage your body becomes one with him.

The Scriptures say, "The two are united into one." But the person who is joined to the Lord becomes one spirit with Him. No other sin so clearly effects the body as this one. Sexual immorality is a sin against your own body. Or don't you know that your body is the temple of the Holy Spirit, who lives in you and was given to you by God?

You do not belong to yourself, for God bought you with a price. So you must honor God with your body. (1 Corinthians 6:15–20)

Notes: Any sexual sin outside of marriage is sin. Fornication, adultery, homosexuality, and sodomy are all sexual sins, and wrong in God's sight.

Other types of wrong soul ties are:
- Co-dependent relationships
- Possessive, controlling relationships
- Occult relationships

Prayer for Breaking Wrong Sexual and/or Soul Ties
Lord, I confess I have sinned against you and my soul and body.
I have misused my body with (name(s)). I repent and am truly sorry for my wrongdoing.
Please forgive me, Lord, and with your help I will sin no more.
I now take the sword of the Spirit and cut each wrong spiritual, physical, mental, and emotional tie between each person with whom I have been wrongfully involved. I seal the ends with the blood of Jesus so they can never be rejoined again.
Thank you, Lord, that these ties no longer have any power over me. I am free in Jesus' name. Amen.

PRAYER FOR CUTTING WRONG GENERATIONAL TIES:

Lord, I take the sword of the spirit, your Word, and cut between the second and third generation the wrong generational tie of (name the wrong spirit: i.e., addictions, rage, etc.) on my father's side and/or my mother's side. I cut that wrong tie and seal the ends with the blood of Jesus Christ never to be joined again. (Continue with this generational cutting prayer next between the first and second generations in either or both sides of the family; then between you and your mother and/or father and finally between you and your children and their children.).

It is finished in this family line. Thank you, Lord. Amen.

Sometimes it is helpful to actually raise your arm as if you are holding a sword and make a cutting motion. You may experience some resistance cutting between certain individuals in your family line. Continue cutting until you feel a release before moving on.

Ephesians 6:13–17:

"Therefore put on the full armor of God, so that when the day of evil comes, you may be able to stand your ground, and after you have done everything, to stand. Stand firm then, with the belt of truth buckled around your waist, with the breastplate of righteousness in place, and with your feet fitted with the readiness that comes from the gospel of peace. In addition to all this, take up the shield of faith, with which you can extinguish all the flaming arrows of the evil one. Take the helmet of salvation and the sword of the Spirit, which is the word of God."

Also see 1 Corinthians 4:8–18

Prayer for pain that does not seem to leave
(From Liberty Savard's book: *The Unsurrendered Soul*, p. 214)

Lord, I bind every cell of my body to your will and purposes for my life. I bind my mind to your mind, Jesus, and I need you to speak to me. I loose, smash, crush, and destroy every effect and influence of word curses being directed toward me. I loose the effects and influences of any witchcraft, voodoo, incantations, and any calling upon demonic forces to attack me. I loose, smash, crush, and destroy any hexes or curses or wrong prayers that have been directed at me. Thank you, Father."

Recite Psalm 64:1–4, 7–8 NIV
Psalm 64

Hear me, my God, as I voice my complaint;
  protect my life from the threat of the enemy.

Hide me from the conspiracy of the wicked,
  from the plots of evildoers.
They sharpen their tongues like swords
  and aim cruel words like deadly arrows.
They shoot from ambush at the innocent;
  they shoot suddenly, without fear.

  But God will shoot them with his arrows;
    they will suddenly be struck down.
  He will turn their own tongues against them
    and bring them to ruin;
  all who see them will shake their heads in scorn.

Repeat if pain returns....

Prayer of Forgiveness from Judgments

Lord, I forgive (name).

Lord, I give you permission to take the judgment and bitterness out of my life.

I do not want this in my life. I surrender it to you, and ask you to remove it, to heal me where I have been wounded . . . to forgive me where I have sinned.

I choose not to blame or hold the actions of others again them. I hereby surrender my right to be paid back for my loss, by the one who has sinned against me, and, in so doing, I declare my trust in God alone, as the Righteous Judge.

Father God, bless them in every way. I ask this in Jesus' name.

Prayers for Renouncing Judgment

"Judgments"

Father, I choose to forgive (my mother, (my father) for (offense). It does not matter if what was done was right or wrong, it was not my place to judge. Please forgive me for my judgment, and I release (name) to you. I ask you to break all ties that hold me to the judgment, in Jesus' name and by His shed blood. Thank you, Father.

Breaking the Power of Word Curses and Inner Vows

A. Breaking the Power of Word Curses:
1. Identify the word curses made against us by others or ourselves. Learn to recognize when a negative forecast is being made, either by you or another.
2. Take authority over the curse in the power and authority of Jesus that resides in us.
3. Bind yourself to Christ and to His promises for our lives. Bind yourself to the truth of His Word (pray specific Scripture verses pertinent to the area of life affected by the curse). Renounce and loose the curse off your life, loosing all the negative effects and the subsequent wrong behaviors, ideas, and beliefs that may have developed (prayer adapted from *Shattering Your Strongholds*, Liberty Savard).
4. Through the blood of Jesus, ask God to forgive us forever making or accepting the word curse. We forgive the others involved and we forgive ourselves.
5. We claim the power of the Holy Spirit as we covenant to walk in victory over the curse.

<u>Important Note</u>:
Breaking the power of the word curse is not the end! Word curses do not exist in a vacuum. Breaking word curses clears some clutter out of the way of healing. After breaking the power, proceed to identifying the root and origin—the memory or situation that is at the root.
Inner healing prayer is effective in finding the open gate that allowed the curse to take root in the soul. Pray for the healing of the wounds caused by unmet needs, unhealed hurts, or unresolved issues and for the revelation of the lies beneath the woundedness. Ask Jesus to bring His truth to nullify the lies and close the gate the lies left open.

6. Proclaim blessings over your life according to God's Word.

B. Breaking Inner vows:
1. **<u>Recognition:</u>** If you don't remember the vow in your conscience mind, the Holy Spirit will reveal them if you ask.
2. **<u>Forgiveness:</u>** Explore and begin the process of forgiving those who have hurt you and yourself. Ask forgiveness of God for judging and taking on His job of Judge.
3. **<u>Confess and repent</u>** of sinful actions that led to the making of the vow.
4. **<u>Renounce the vow:</u>** Vows can be broken by the authority given us by Jesus Christ. Use the authority of binding and loosing (Mt. 16:19; 18:18). You may also be led by the Holy Spirit to speak to an inner child part that needs to be released from the vow.
5. Tell the Lord you are **<u>ready and willing to accept the gifts</u>** He has been waiting to give you (or the one prayed with).
6. **<u>Persevere:</u>** We must overcome long-practiced habits.

It is important to recognize that (like word curses) inner vows do not exist in a vacuum. They come about because of a hurtful experience. The above process of renouncing is most powerful and effective in the course of the inner healing of the memories and feelings of that event.

If you uncover an inner vow, be sure to **go to the root and origin of that inner vow** for Jesus to bring inner healing to that experience. It is the encounter with Him that provides healing. Until healing is at the depth of experience, we are in danger of merely supplying more information to the person. That may bring temporary relief, but it won't bring healing.

Inner Vows Prayer:

In the name of Jesus, I renounce the vow I made (<u>state vow</u>). I repent of it and break it by the power of Jesus name and His shed blood. Please forgive me, Father, and set me free from the effects of that vow. Thank you, Father. Amen.

PSALM 23 Meditation

The Lord is my shepherd, my pastor, my supplier, I shall not want anything. . .
He makes me to lie down in green, living pastures:
He leads me beside the still, peaceful waters that heal. . .
He restores my soul: my mind, my will, and my emotions.
He leads me in paths of righteousness, of being in right relationship with Him and others
For his name's sake . . .
Yea, though I walk, not crawl or heavily trod, through the valley of the
Shadow of death, for it is only a shadow, not the real thing, I will fear no evil:
For you are with me: You are always with me. Your rod of authority and your staff of love and mercy,
They comfort me.
You prepare a table before me in the presence of my enemies: a feasting banquet right in the wilderness you have
prepared for me. You anoint my
Head with oil: Your healing oil, so much that my cup runs over.
Surely, goodness, the very goodness of you and your mercy, your unfailing mercy, shall follow me
all the days of my life: and on this earth and the kingdom to come I will dwell in the
House of the LORD forever.

The Body

THE BODY, THE BREAD WAS BROKEN
THE BLOOD, THE WINE WAS POURED.
ONE BY ONE SINGLE FILE THEY CAME
THE FAITHFUL AND THE FAITH-FILLED
THE DOUBTER AND THE QUESTIONER
THE ISOLATED AND THE EMBRACED
THE LONELY AND THE LOVELY
THE HURTING AND THE HEALED.
ELDER AND YOUNGER
MALE AND FEMALE
BELIEVER AND DOUBTER
SOULS ON FIRE
HEARTS OF STONE.
SENSUOUSLY CLOSE
FRIGHTENINGLY DISTANT
EXPECTANT
REDEEMED SANCTIFIED FORGIVEN LOVED
"The Chalice" HCB '98

"Yielding Will to God and Cleansing Imagination Prayer"

Dear Father God,

I yield my will to you. I give you permission to go to any level within me, to heal, cleanse, and restore according to your truth.

To the best of my ability I invite you to be my Lord, unconditionally. Please be Lord of my subconscious, as well as my conscious mind.

I renounce every false teaching and attitude, and ask you to cleanse and protect me with Jesus' blood.

I cast down every wrong imagination and everything that exalts itself against the Knowledge of God, and I bring every thought captive to the Lord Jesus Christ.

(2 Corinthians 10:5, personalized)

Thank you, Lord God, in Jesus' Name.

CHAPTER 9

Walking Out Your Healing In Daily Victory

Key Concepts:
- Healing is a process
- God initiates and completes the process
- Need for Christian community
- Use the tools of Bible study and prayer and find a mentor or spiritual director

Introduction:

Walking in daily victory in healing is the process of being sanctified. Spiritual victory comes through a continually renewed relationship with God. Your relationship with God needs to remain new and fresh. Our salvation is assured because of our personal acceptance of Jesus Christ as our Lord and Savior. The challenge of Christian living is to walk in victory daily. *"...continue to work out your salvation with fear and trembling."* (Philippians 2:12)

"As you have therefore received Christ Jesus the Lord, so walk in Him, rooted and built up in Him and established in the faith, as you have been taught, abounding in it with thanksgiving." (Colossians 2:6-7)

Healing is a Process

Sometimes it seems in healing that we take three steps forward and two back. Healing is a process. Scripture states "I AM the God who heals you" (Exodus 15:26) This simple verse challenges Christians to not trivialize healing by quick answers when healing seems to fail or be a struggle or by diminishing God's divine work because the modern world seeks natural explanations or by insisting that human criteria are met in our evaluation of the sustainability of healing. Many Christians, especially in North America, want quick solutions and fast healing. Perseverance, patience, and deeper revelation of healing have been and remain challenges in inner healing.

Healing is a divine work and because this is so, it is difficult to evaluate the sustainability of inner healing as evidenced by transformed lives through Christ reflecting new behavior. It is difficult because we look at healing through human eyes. Relapse, a modern term, is like backsliding, falling, or stumbling, as described in Scripture (Hebrews 6:4-6). We do fall and God, who is the Healer, calls us back again and again. Nothing is impossible for God. This brings hope to all who struggle or may relapse in the healing process.

Someone I prayed with who was struggling with her self-centeredness that continued to plague her stated her goal in healing: *"I would also like to be able to regard the person who may be causing me pain, with love, instead of having my awareness focused on myself (Other-centered vs. self-centered).* She had not lost hope in this struggle.

The theologian Karl Barth states "The last word concerning the world of men is not 'Dust thou art and unto dust shalt thou return!' But, because I live, ye shall live also. With this last word in our minds we feel hope and our need stirring within us. The advancing glory of God has already vouchsafed us" (Barth 297).

God initiates and completes the process

Scripture clearly declares God is the alpha and the omega and so it is with healing. This realization is not just words but revelation or epiphany. God is faithful and steadfast! And He gives us the power to be faithful and steadfast.

Perhaps a better definition of healing has to do with this steadfastness in going on despite difficulty or delay in achieving success. Does healing and living out that healing in spite of setbacks, mean all of us in the healing process are to remain steadfast, devoted to God and who He is, not fearful, and giving Him our undivided attention no matter what? None of us are perfected in any of this. This is the messiness or the loose ends of trying to define healing. One person in the healing process succinctly states this: "I must know I can trust God and not fear that the negative behavior pattern will continue. I can either choose the way of fear or way of love." Again we hear Philip Melanchthon "What the heart desires, the will chooses, and the mind justifies," for healing or destruction (Allison 128-129).

Need for Christian Community

The need for Christian community as a support for participants involved in inner healing is crucial for one's success and well-being. Community gives us all the opportunity to share with each other with great transparency the difficulties of maintaining healing. It is astounding and delightful to hear another verbalize your own struggle with life issues like identity and insecurity. It is also encourageing to hear another's victory over walking out ones healing.

Martin Luther, suffered from severe bouts of depression throughout his life. As I studied his life it became apparent the need for community support and compassion. These bouts of depression in Luther's life which brought him into a devastating aloneness and absolute negation of himself were the ashes from which the heart of his lectures and sermons rose bringing many to hear him. At one point during a time of experiencing terrible night terrors he wrote, "'...I will defy Duke George and all the lawyers and theologians, but when these knaves, the spirits of evil come, the Church must join in the fight...'" (Todd 343). The Church must join in the fight of healing and deliverance with one another.

If you want to grow in your Christian walk you must have committed relationships with other Christians. We need other Christians who will hold us accountable for progress on our healing journey. Why? Because we are easily deceived. We don't always see ourselves clearly. We need safe places to share. We need others to love us up close and personal. Our communities must become healing communities where others can look at us and say, "See how they love one another." We have to spend time with people to build deep relationships.

Tools

Personal scripture study is crucial for the development of our inner being. We must take our experiences and match them with the Word of God to trust their authenticity. Our experiences should form God's character in us. His Word is sharper than a two-edged sword. It will separate from your life ungodly things. If you do not know the Word how will you be guided? How will you know who is speaking to you? All scripture is God-breathed. (Timothy 3:16). "Be washed by the water of the Word," (Ephesians 5:26).

Pray the scriptures (1 Thessalonians 5:23-24). Let the Word dwell, come to life, in you (Colossians 3:16). The Word of God changes you (Romans 2:4).

Discover your gifts and allow the Holy Spirit to use them in service of others.

Spend time with God every day.

Share your healing with others. Pour out the mercy you've received out on someone else. Pouring out what you have received redeems your pain. Learn how to pray inner healing prayer with others. So many are wounded and need healing.

Grow in responsibility to your community. Where are you spending your time? Your money? Your talent? Are your resources being spent on reaching unbelievers?

In Conclusion:

Remember that the healing process is more cyclic than linear in structure. Charles Spurgeon's reference to sanctification by participation of the Holy Ghost, succinctly points to this process of healing. Healings allow deeper penetration within, newly exposing our natural defects as well as hidden wounds not healed yet. The struggles in maintaining healing demonstrate the struggle for sanctified souls between grace and corruption. And through it all God is with us every day, every minute of our lives! Emmanuel!

WALKNG OUT HEALING PRAYER

Thank you Lord for the healing and your love and compassion for me. You have given me tools and knowledge to continue walking out my healing.

I present to you my soul and my body as a living sacrifice. Lord, I give you permission to crucify my sinful nature daily in order that I may have your character built into me. I give you all my anxiety and fears in exchange for your peace and perfect love.

Holy Spirit be my teacher. Daily show me the way of truth and love. Teach me how to serve you and others. Teach me how to surrender my plans and instead receive your plans for my life each day. Renew my mind and heart. Show me how to be a godly friend. (If married how to be a godly spouse and parent.). Help me to make good heathy decisions about my body. Bring me into deeper relationship with you and teach me how to worship you and pray to you. When I fail, show me your mercy, your truth and how much you love me. Help me to daily walk with you and with your help, daily walk out my healing. Amen.

Recommended Reading and Works Consulted

Allender, Dr. Dan B. *The Wounded Heart: Hope for the Victims of Childhood Sexual Abuse.* Colorado Springs: Navpress, 1990. Print.

The Archbishop's Council. *A Time to Heal: A Report for the House of Bishops on the Healing Ministry.* Trowbridge, Wiltshire: Cromwell, 2000. Print.

Augsburger, David W. *Helping People Forgive.* Louisville: Westminster John Knox Press, 1996. Print.

Bennett, Rita. *Emotionally Free.* North Brunswick: Bridge-Logos Publishers, 1982. Print.

Bosworth, F. F. *Christ the Healer.* Grand Rapids: Revell, 1973, 2000, 9th ed. Print.

Flynn, Mike and Doug Gregg. *Inner Healing.* Downers Grove, Illinois: InterVarsity Press. 1993. Print.

Gockel, Annemarie. "Spirituality and the Process of Healing: A Narrative Study." *The International Journal for the Psychology of Religion 19* (2009): 217–230. Print.

Guyon, Jeanne. *Song of Songs.* New Kensington: Whitaker House, 1997. Print.

House, Wayne H. ed. *Divorce and Remarriage: Four Christian Views.* Downers Grove: InterVarsity, 1990. Print.

Ilibagiza, Immaculee. *Left to Tell.* Carlsbad: Hay House, 2006. Print.

Kalsched, Donald. *The Inner World of Trauma.* New York: Brunner-Routledge, 1996. Print.

Kraft, Charles H. *Deep Wounds, Deep Healing.* Ann Arbor: Vine Books/Servant Pub., 1993. Print.

Kylstra, Chester, and Betsy Kylstra. *Restoring the Foundations: An Integrated Approach to Healing Ministry.* Hendersonville: Proclaiming His Word Pub., 2001. 2nd ed. Print.

Linn, Matthew and Dennis Linn. *Healing Life's Hurts: Healing of Memories through Five Stages of Forgiveness.* New York: Paulist P, 1978. Print.

MacNutt, Francis. *Healing.* University of Notre Dame: Ave Maria Press. 1974. Print.

May, Gerald G. *Addiction and Grace.* San Francisco: Harper & Row, 1988. Print.

Meyendorff, Paul. *The Anointing of the Sick.* New York: St. Vladimir's Seminary P, 2009. Print.

Monroe, Philip G., George M. Schwab. "God as Healer: A Closer Look at Biblical Images of Inner Healing with Guiding Questions for Counselors." *Journal of Psychology and Christianity* 28.2 (2009): 121–129. Print.

Mumford, Nigel. *After the Trauma the Battle Begins.* Troy, NY: Troy Book Makers, 2011. Print.

Newbigin, Lesslie. *The Household of God.* New York: Friendship P, 1954. Print.

Packer, J. I. *Knowing God.* Downers Grove: InterVarsity, 1993. Print.

Payne, Leanne. *The Broken Image.* Westchester: Crossway Books, 1981. Print.

———. *The Healing Presence: Curing the Soul Through Union with Christ.* Grand Rapids: Baker Books, 1995. Print.

———. *Restoring the Christian Soul: Overcoming Barriers to Completion in Christ Through Healing Prayer.* Grand Rapids: Baker Books, 1996. Print.

Pearson, Mark. *Christian Healing: A Practical and Comprehensive Guide.* Orlando, FL: Creation House, 2004. Print.

Reichenbach, Bruce R. "By His Stripes We Are Healed." *Journal of the Evangelical Theological Society* 41:4 (1998): 551–560. Print.

Sanford, John and Paula. *The Transformation of the Inner Man.* Tulsa: Victory House, 1982. Print.

Savard, Liberty. *Shattering Your Strongholds.* Gainesville: Bridge-Logos, 1992. Print.

———. *The Unsurrendered Soul.* Gainesville: Bridge-Logos, 2002. Print.

Smith, Cheryl. "Substance Abuse, Chronic Sorrow, and Mothering Loss: Relapse Triggers Among Female Victims of Child Abuse." *Pediatric Nursing* 24.5 (2009): 401-412. Print.

Smith , Ed M. *Beyond Tolerable Recovery.* Campbellsville: Alathia Pub., 1999. Print.

Stapleton, Ruth Carter. *The Experience of Inner Healing.* Waco: Word, 1977. Print.

Stott, John R. W. *The Cross of Christ.* Downers Grove: InterVarsity, 1986. Print.

Todd, John M. *Luther: A Life.* New York: Cross Road, 1982. Print.

Torrance, Thomas F. *Theology in Reconciliation.* Grand Rapids: Eerdmans, 1976. Print.

Volf, Miroslav. *The End of Memory: Remembering Rightly in a Violent World.* Grand Rapids: Eerdmans, 2006. Print.

Wang, Shirley. "Can You Alter Your Memory?" *The Wall Street Journal* (15 March 2010): 3. Print.

Wright, Christopher J. H. *The Mission of God: Unlocking the Bible's Grand Narrative.* Downers Grove: InterVarsity, 2006. Print.

Wright, Dr. H. Norman. *Crisis & Trauma Counseling.* Ventura: Regal, 2003. Print.

Wright, N. T. *Scripture and the Authority of God.* London: SPCK, 2005. Print.

Yoder, Carolyn. *Trauma Healing.* Intercourse: Good Books, 2005. Print.